Survival Guide for
New Campus Administrators

■ ■ ■

Survival Guide for New Campus Administrators

How to Become a Professional, Effective, and Successful Administrator

■ ■ ■

Laura Trujillo-Jenks and Minerva Trujillo

Park Place Publications, L.P.
Austin, Texas

Park Place Publications, L.P.
1601 Rio Grande, Suite 455
Austin, Texas 78701
(512) 478-2113 • Fax: (512) 495-9955
www.legaldigest.com

First Printing: May 2013

ISBN 978-0-9833083-9-3

To Kenny, my best friend
—Laura

To Arthur, my loving husband of 41 years
—Minerva

■ ■ ■

Contents

Introduction

Survival Guide for New Campus Administrators imparts knowledge that we have gathered in our combined 50 years in education. These years have been good to us because we have learned what it takes to lead a school campus, while understanding various rules, policies, and laws. We are excited about sharing this knowledge in order to help others be the best administrators possible, so that their teachers and students can be successful.

This nontechnical, straightforward book is divided into three parts: Leading through Teaching and Learning, Leading through Data-Driven Decisions, and Leading with Vigilance. In the first part, three chapters focus on how campus leaders must be grounded in instruction and curriculum. Chapter 1 covers concepts related to curriculum and instruction and discusses teaching tenets, collaboration, discipline gurus, and special programs. Various types of traditional and nontraditional instructional settings are highlighted in chapter 2, with helpful hints on how to work in each setting. The third chapter presents the typical administrative hierarchy within a school district and provides concise explanations of the roles and duties of the assorted personnel in the school district's central offices and on school campuses.

The second part of the book, "Leading through Data-Driven Decisions," centers on accountability, finance, and partnerships. Chapter 4 describes what accountability means for administrators, teachers, students, and parents. It also includes a plan of action for handling conflicts. The next chapter, on campus finance and budgets, gives tips on how to handle the different types of funds assigned to a campus and how to stay legal when it comes to money allocated to a campus. The last chapter in this section involves partnerships with parents and community. Included are steps to increase both parental and community involvement and examples of what can be accomplished through such partnerships.

The last part of the book, "Leading with Vigilance," focuses on keeping a school safe and secure, plus a final chapter of tips on leading a campus. Chapter 7 details how to keep a school safe and secure and includes a section on security personnel and their function in helping to maintain a secure campus. The next chapter explains how to create and implement crisis plans and reviews troublesome issues that campuses currently face. The concluding chapter is full of practical advice that administrators will want to incorporate into their leadership style. The appendices include a helpful chart of the many types of special programs within school districts and on campuses, plus excerpts from federal and state statutory codes as examples of the types of codes that campus administrators must be familiar with and abide by.

All administrators will find this book to be a valuable resource, but it is especially designed for brand-new administrators. Coming from the classroom into a role that holds high expectations and many responsibilities may be invigorating, yet overwhelming and confusing. If you are a new or aspiring administrator, take the time to learn what it means to be a successful and effective campus leader, and strive to understand all that your school district expects. Finally, love what you do! Find enjoyment in every task you perform as an educational administrator. If you enjoy your job, then you will help create a happy school where success is inevitable.

Note on Terminology

The word "staff" is used frequently in this book to denote all personnel who work on a campus, including teachers, secretaries, aides, maintenance and cafeteria workers, and anyone else who is a paid employee on your campus. When specificity is needed, personnel are described by their particular positions. Additionally, the campus staff is sometimes referred to as the campus family.

Leading through Teaching and Learning

■ ■ ■

Chapter 1

The Curriculum and Instructional Leader

The first realization a new principal has of what it takes to be a curriculum and instructional leader is the vast amount of reading, listening, and observing that is required. Studying the state-approved curriculum and finding out how it aligns with grade levels and disciplines is necessary for all new administrators, so that they will understand what kinds of teaching will be occurring in the classrooms. This chapter will guide you in recognizing what you already know as a teacher and conceptualizing it in your role as a new administrator.

What Are Curriculum and Instruction?

First, before delving into the various layers of responsibilities that a new administrator will encounter, it is important to understand what a curriculum and instructional leader is and how being an effective one will help you manage your campus. Second, a clear distinction must be made between the terms "curriculum" and "instruction." The curriculum can be thought of as a road map that teachers use to lead their students to a major student learning objective (SLO) in a given subject at a given grade level (see the illustration on page 4). The main route has side streets to explore—subtopics and sub-SLOs that enhance the main SLO by helping students understand, learn, and transfer the concepts from one discipline to others, as well as to real-life situations. Along the way, an overpass may be encountered—another discipline that shares certain components, such as SLOs, that are taught from a different angle. Using like concepts to teach two or more subjects or disciplines—math and science, for example—is called interdisciplinary teaching.

The curriculum road map is created by a committee at the national or state level, depending on what the state's education department develops and deems as the accepted curriculum. At the local school district level, the accepted curriculum is followed, but it may be enhanced through a scope and sequence document, curriculum guides, and shared lesson plans. In most cases,

Curriculum Road Map
Social Studies: The American Revolution

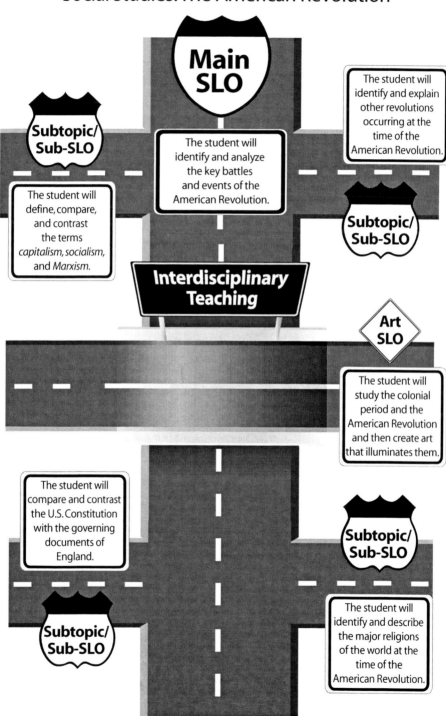

Main SLO

The student will identify and analyze the key battles and events of the American Revolution.

Subtopic/ Sub-SLO

The student will define, compare, and contrast the terms *capitalism, socialism,* and *Marxism.*

The student will identify and explain other revolutions occurring at the time of the American Revolution.

Subtopic/ Sub-SLO

Interdisciplinary Teaching

Art SLO

The student will study the colonial period and the American Revolution and then create art that illuminates them.

The student will compare and contrast the U.S. Constitution with the governing documents of England.

Subtopic/ Sub-SLO

Subtopic/ Sub-SLO

The student will identify and describe the major religions of the world at the time of the American Revolution.

the curriculum includes several levels of complexity for each idea, concept, or objective, so that teachers can make adjustments for individual students' needs and students can learn cumulatively. Instruction, then, is how the curriculum is relayed to students. It is what lesson plans are made of and what a teacher actually does in the classroom to present the curriculum. For example, if the eighth-grade curriculum in social studies states that students will learn about the American Revolution, then the instruction may include having the students write an essay or "book" about a certain event during the Revolution or having the class reenact a battle. The instruction brings the curriculum to a level that a student will understand, internalize, and then transfer to other subjects.

All administrators should have a thorough understanding of the mandated curriculum, because it is what must be taught in the classrooms. An additional purpose of the curriculum is to prepare students to take state assessments, which are "graded" and published as campus, district, and state report cards. Hence, your knowledge of the curriculum and delivery of instruction on your campus will help you in many situations; for example, when a parent asks you about a SLO, you will be prepared to answer thoughtfully. Furthermore, many school administrators are evaluated on how effective the campus's teachers are in following the curriculum and ensuring student success, and this evaluation is included on the campus report card.

The Teaching Tenets

So what should instruction look like in the classroom if a teacher is following the curriculum? The answer to this question is essential to recognizing good and bad instruction on a campus. As you study your district's approved evaluation components and apply them to the way teachers deliver instruction, you will learn to decipher good instruction from bad.

Knowing the key components of good instruction—the teaching tenets— will help you tell whether or not you are observing good instruction. Keep in mind that, even in good teaching, some of these components will not always be present, however. Depending on the time of the year (assessment time or beginning/end of the school year, for example) or other circumstances (such as death of a student or teacher), teachers may find teachable moments that will change the day's instruction. But ordinarily you should expect to see these tenets often throughout a school year when you are visiting classrooms.

> ***Rapport and classroom environment***—A teacher's knowledge of the abilities of his or her students can be more easily seen if good rapport has been built between them. This rapport will also help a teacher

understand students' strengths and weaknesses and how to differentiate and individualize instruction for each student. A good relationship between a teacher and students also promotes a healthy classroom environment, which will be reflected in good personal interactions between the teacher and the students when you visit a classroom. Look for students working together and understanding the teacher's expectations the first time they are given. If you notice instead that students are confused or are not familiar with the way a teacher is behaving, then you may be witnessing a dog and pony show.

Differentiation of instruction—A relatively new term for an old habit of some teachers, "differentiation of instruction" means finding out what the needs of each student are and then providing instruction that meets those needs. This differentiation should be apparent in the lesson plans, but you should also see it when you are visiting classrooms and listening to teachers and students converse. Variety in student products, like a written test for one student and an oral test for another, is a good sign of differentiation of instruction. Also, look at the student work that sometimes is hanging on the walls or is on the students' desks. Observe what each student is doing to demonstrate that he or she understands the instruction being given.

Individualization—Individualization is similar to differentiation. A teacher differentiates instruction by teaching individual students differently, according to their needs. With individualization, a teacher also ensures that each student receives accommodations (leveling the playing field) and/or modifications (changing the shape of the playing field by changing the curriculum, instruction, and assessment). Your teachers who work with special populations will know how to individualize, because each of those students will have an individualized education program (IEP) or a limited English proficiency (LEP) plan, for example, that is specific for him or her. As an administrator, you must read about and understand the types of accommodations and modifications that may be in place for any student in any classroom, so that you do not unfairly question why a teacher is allowing one student to do something that others aren't doing. For example, an accommodation might be to allow a student to use a magnifying glass when reading, and a modification might be to have a student work on an SLO that is entirely different from the SLO for the majority of the class.

Rigor and meaningful learning—Challenges (rigor) and value (meaningful learning) are the hallmarks of encouraging students to learn. Teachers who incorporate rigor and meaningful learning into their lessons push their students academically to learn and appreciate the content. Challenges are seen when students are purposefully made to work outside their comfort zone, and value is seen when students can relate what they are learning to what is important to them. The inclusion of this tenet will be evident if a teacher is teaching critical thinking skills through the application of Bloom's Taxonomy or Erickson's Structure of Knowledge. (For information on these classification systems for learning and teaching, see "References and Recommended Resources" at the end of this book.)

Interesting, engaging, and motivational teaching—An interesting lesson is one that captures the students' attention and generates a desire to learn more about a topic. Engaging lessons get students involved through application and creation. Motivational lessons inspire students and move them to care about learning the topic at hand. Students who are excited about going to class, who can answer your questions substantially when asked what they learned in class that day, and who are motivated to come to school to learn are clear signs that a teacher is providing interesting, engaging, and motivational lessons.

Variation through Multisensory Learning—Learning can occur through auditory, visual, kinesthetic, and tactile means, and students differ in the type of sensory learning that works best for them. Teachers who are aware of how their students learn will understand how to vary lessons through multisensory activities. Although this type of learning may not take place every day and all day, teachers who vary their instructional delivery in this way not only help students learn and retain knowledge but also find that teaching can be fun and fulfilling.

Transferability and connections to other disciplines—Making connections to other disciplines and instilling in students the ability to transfer knowledge from one course to another or from one life situation to another should be main objectives of all teachers. Teachers who co-teach and purposefully work to connect concepts of one discipline with concepts of another discipline strengthen the learning process.

You should see evidence of these teaching tenets frequently when you observe a classroom. They should be obvious and clear, and if they are not, then don't be afraid to ask the teachers and students about how the tenets are incorporated into their daily lessons and instruction. Their insight and perspective may help shape your perception of what you are observing. It will also give the teacher and students a chance to tell you what *they* are observing, providing you with further data for making a professional judgment on how a teacher is performing in the classroom.

The Good, the Bad, and the Exceptional

When you visit a classroom, it is best to start with the assumption that you will be observing good instruction. What does good teaching look like, and how can you tell the master teachers from the proficient teachers? This question will become easier to answer as you practice observing teachers and their delivery of instruction.

In this book, a master teacher is one who consistently and constantly instructs students who successfully understand and internalize the curriculum. The proof of this student success can be found in achievement tests, state assessments, IQ tests, graduation rates, and any college entry-level test. Master teachers usually make up no more than 5 to 10 percent of the teaching staff. Most teachers are proficient teachers, skilled in teaching the curriculum and seeing much student success and achievement. These teachers are comfortable in performing the many tasks assigned to them, and they incorporate the teaching tenets most of the time and efficiently.

Good teaching, then, is most likely what you will see in many of the classrooms that are on your campus. You will see students engaged, motivated, and transferring knowledge from one classroom to the next. You will also see teachers who have good rapport with their students and who really care about doing a good job instructing students. For the most part, observing good teaching will be the norm for you. As long as you see implementation of the teaching tenets and fulfillment of your school district expectations for teachers, what you observe will be good teaching.

Keep in mind that not all teachers are the same and will not teach in the same way. Two teachers will deliver the same lesson differently and with their own flair. Teachers have individual ideas of how to deliver instruction and how to instruct using the teaching tenets. Therefore, you must leave your biases and prejudices at the door, because not all teachers will teach the way you did when you were teaching. If you liked teaching with collaborative grouping and using manipulatives in each lesson when you were a teacher, don't judge the teachers you evaluate by the same criteria. Their unique styles will be illuminated as you consistently observe them. Learn what each teacher does on your campus, and why, so that you can give all of them a fair evaluation.

If you are coming from an elementary teaching background and find yourself leading at a secondary school (or vice versa), what qualifies as good teaching may be very different from what you are used to observing. For example, if you taught a core subject, like English, and now you have to appraise fine arts teachers, you will discover that fine arts teachers do not teach the same way English teachers do. A band director will do much lecturing and modeling with a first-year band class and will not allow much student collaboration at the start of the year, whereas an English teacher may do the opposite. An art teacher may allow sharp objects, such as scissors and X-Acto knives, to be used to create art and may allow students to converse with each other while working. If this kind of teaching does not conform to the way you did things as an English teacher, then ask the teachers why they teach the way they do and how their teaching style helps students succeed. Try not to jump to conclusions about whether or not you are observing good teaching. Give teachers ample time and opportunities to show you that they are incorporating the teaching tenets, and follow up by reviewing your school's report card and past teacher evaluations to confirm what you are seeing. However, before viewing past teacher evaluations, form your own opinion about a teacher, based on observable facts.

Now that we have an idea of the elements of good teaching, what does bad teaching look like? You might think that bad teaching would be easier to detect, but if you allow your biases and preconceptions to get in the way of an objective view of a teacher, then you may see more bad teaching than good. Essentially, bad teaching results when a teacher refuses to follow the teaching tenets and the expectations of the school and school district. This type of teacher may refuse guidance toward correcting delivery of instruction or may not know how to integrate the teaching tenets into lessons. Bad teaching may also occur when a teacher is overwhelmed and needs assistance.

Bad teaching can definitely be shifted to good teaching, and that is where you, as the curriculum and instructional leader, must step in. It is ultimately your job to ensure that your teachers are successful, because if they are, then their students will be successful, and you in turn will be too. When you were a teacher, you wanted your students to flourish and achieve; the same goes for you as the leader of a campus. Because you will want your teachers to succeed, you may need to ensure that they receive professional development or any other guidance that will help them become more proficient.

Transforming bad teaching into good will require some work on your part. You will need to take an active role in helping struggling teachers improve their teaching, by consistently observing them and giving them pointers on how to succeed. The following steps are recommended:

1. Get to know the areas in which a teacher is struggling by observing the teacher deliver instruction.

2. Talk to the teacher about these areas and offer the teacher an opportunity to tell you which areas he or she feels overwhelmed by, and why.

3. Together, work on a plan of action that lists exactly what areas of improvement are needed and what activities will be done to strengthen these areas. These activities may include professional development, visits to a master teacher's classroom, and one-on-one weekly conferences with you. Also, discuss how the teacher's strong areas can be used to strengthen the weak ones.

4. Choose no more than three areas of improvement for the action plan. Once the teacher strengthens those areas, other areas of improvement can be added as needed.

5. Create a timeline for the plan so that both of you will know when improvement goals are expected to be reached.

6. Revisit the action plan at a predetermined time, revamping it or closing it, depending on the teacher's progress.

In some schools, an action plan like this one is called a growth plan or a plan for a teacher in need of assistance. This kind of plan should be seen, not as a negative, but as an opportunity for a teacher to be successful. Work with struggling teachers to help them learn how to become more proficient and to enjoy the profession they have chosen.

Leading, Teaching, and Learning

Leading a school offers so many promising possibilities, especially when an administrator realizes that some teachers are eager to lead while also teaching and learning. This means that an administrator must teach teachers the expectations of curriculum and instruction. An administrator must also be ready to learn from teachers, especially those who are seen as gurus or master teachers. This mutual teaching and learning should include the understanding of "C-I-A," collaboration, gurus on campus, and special programs.

C-I-A

Curriculum and instruction are two parts of a trilogy that also includes assessment, or C-I-A. Because the curriculum is usually mandated at the federal or state level, all school districts and schools must follow it. The curriculum can be changed *only* if a special education committee meeting agrees that it should and develops an individualized education program (IEP) for a particular student. Otherwise, the curriculum must be taught as written and may not be supplanted with any other curriculum that is not aligned with the federal and state expectations and approved.

Instruction, however, is usually not mandated and is at the teacher's discretion. Teachers may choose the instructional means they will use for translating the curriculum into meaningful learning for students. That is why the teaching tenets and the teacher evaluation system are so important: they show whether and how a teacher is implementing the teaching tenets and whether students are successful. In some cases, a school district or school campus will buy an instructional program and mandate its use, but even then, teachers are still able to present it using their unique instructional style.

Horizontal and Vertical Collaboration

Good teaching can be emphasized and even structured through both horizontal and vertical collaboration, or professional learning communities (PLCs). A horizontal PLC meeting involves teachers of the same grade level, of the same discipline, and/or whose students who have the same need (such as special education), and they discuss the important elements for student success. For example, a fifth-grade-level collaborative team may consist of a science teacher, an English teacher, a social studies teacher, and a math teacher who meet weekly or monthly to discuss lesson plans, student success, and upcoming school events.

A vertical PLC is similar, but it involves teachers from different grade levels who are teaching the same discipline or subject. The vertical team usually talks about the alignment of the curriculum with grade levels and how the progression of concepts and objectives should be taught. This team may also discuss what students in each grade are expected to know before entering the next grade level.

Gurus and Instructional Specialists

Each campus has a group of gurus who are experts on a special program or master teachers in their discipline. Usually at least one guru may be found in each core discipline, fine arts department, foreign language classroom, and so on. These specialists can make your job as the campus curriculum and instructional leader easier, because it is not humanly possible for a new administrator to know and understand each and every discipline and the curriculum focus for each academic area. Hence, find those gurus who are willing to explain what the teachers in their discipline do and why. Take the time to get to know these gurus, and respect that they know their field well.

Don't be embarrassed to ask these experts questions and to show humility by observing what they do in order to learn about their discipline. For example, many administrators make the mistake of not asking questions about certain curricula—such as the college-readiness system AVID (Advancement Via Individual Determination)—and then will lower their evaluation of a teacher for not teaching in the way they expected. Understanding what AVID is and how an AVID teacher must deliver instruction will help you appraise and evaluate a teacher fairly.

Gurus are found among district-level heads and directors too. Seek these persons out, because they can help you understand state and federal regulations that encompass the special programs they lead. They will also have information about how to implement a special program on a campus and what to expect from teachers who are tasked with following a specialized curriculum.

Special Programs

Special programs encompass many different instructional settings for helping qualified students who need a specialized curriculum. Federal and state mandates describe how special programs will function, so understanding each special program that is housed on the campus you lead is paramount. Leaders are expected to conduct special program meetings in which a committee makes decisions on behalf of a student. Paperwork from these meetings may include an individualized education program (IEP), an academic enhancement plan (AEP), modifications, and/or accommodations.

Special programs have requirements or criteria that participants must meet. Some programs are only for qualified high school juniors and seniors. Other programs specify that a participant must be a first-generation college student or economically disadvantaged. Still others simply require that a student attend a certain school. A list of special programs, with program descriptions, explanations of who qualifies, and what campus leaders must know, is provided in appendix A. For more information about each of these programs, visit the U.S. Department of Education website at www.ed.gov, and type the name of the program in the search box. Your state education agency's website will also have information about these programs as they pertain to your state.

One common special program that is usually located on most campuses within a school district is special education. Mandated under the Individuals with Disabilities Education Act (IDEA), special education happens to be one of the most litigious special programs, so school administrators must be familiar with it. This relatively young program, established in 1975 through the Education for All Handicapped Children Act (Public Law 94-142), is the most powerful law supporting a special program. It has given parents the power to sue schools for any seeming misdeed, such as not implementing an IEP per the parents' understanding.

Special education has many aspects and layers that may seem overwhelming and confusing to administrators. That is one reason some administrators dread going to IEP meetings and making decisions that could land them in court. Additionally, administrators who are not familiar with special education tend to acquiesce to parents unconditionally, putting strains and unrealistic pressure on teachers. *Do not become that kind of administrator.* Instead, learn all you can about what special education is and about the laws that govern it.

Special Education Terminology

Below are some terms and definitions that will help you understand the basics of special education.

- *FAPE*—Free Appropriate Public Education is a right of children with disabilities to an education that is free of monetary charge and appropriate for their level of learning. FAPE is of outmost importance in special education. No matter how expensive materials become or how many teachers are assigned in order to provide special education services to a child, all will be free of charge and appropriate to the child's needs.

- *Medical services and related services*—Medical services are anything that must be provided by a nurse or a doctor. A related service is anything that any layperson, who is trained, may do to serve a child, like tube feeding or catheterization.

- *Child Find*—States are required to identify and evaluate children with disabilities, from birth to age three, in order to provide early intervention as needed. This system is called Child Find. School districts assign someone to be a Child Find liaison, and this person visits hospitals, pediatrician offices, day care centers, and other facilities and reminds district personnel of the need to identify, locate, and evaluate children and families who could benefit from special education services.

- *Committee decision*—*Any plan or change* that pertains to a child in special education requires a committee decision. No person or group may make a unilateral decision about changes to a student's educational plan or IEP paperwork.

- *Discipline*—Students in special education *must* follow the school board–approved student code of conduct (SCOC). They should *never* be allowed to ignore the SCOC, and its rules and consequences should never be relaxed for special education students. However, make sure you know the guidelines for disciplining special education students. For example, when suspending a student in special education, the magic period to remember is 10 days. Students in general education may be suspended for as many days as needed throughout the school year, but a student in special education may be suspended no more than 10 days for the whole year. Because some students are persistent rule breakers, 10 days may not be enough. If special education services are provided during days of suspension, however, then those days don't count toward the 10 days. So if you do need to place a child on out-of-school or in-school suspension, be sure that special education services, including transportation services, are provided each day of the suspension, so that you will have more flexibility in applying suspensions when they are called for.

- *FBA and BIP*—At times, a functional behavioral assessment (FBA) and a behavior intervention plan (BIP) are needed for a student with discipline and behavior issues. An FBA is completed by teachers, parents, administrators, and anyone else who provides services for the student. This information, which is then pooled into one document, describes the behaviors that are to be extinguished or lessened. Precipitators to each undesired behavior are listed along with what occurs during and after the behavior. Additionally, the time a student starts and ends the undesired behavior is listed. From the FBA, the BIP is developed. This plan will include at least three behaviors to be extinguished or lessened with positive interventions listed. For example, if a student shouts out profanity during class, a positive intervention by the teacher could be to praise all of the students who are not using profanity and to give them a treat. The BIP is intended to supplement the SCOC and never to supplant it. It is to be used as a positive way to help students with behavior problems to abide by the SCOC and behave accordingly.

- *Section 504*—Also referred to simply as "504," Section 504 is *not* the same as special education. General education students who qualify under Section 504 receive services similar to those that a special education student receives. A child must have both a diagnosed disability *and* an educational need in order to receive special education services, whereas to qualify for 504, a child must have a medical ailment or condition (cancer or asthma, for example) that severely impairs a life activity, like attending school and learning.

- *Response to Intervention*—RtI is an early intervention program and is not a part of special education. It is a three- to five-tier program to help students become academically and/or behaviorally successful. Through intensive strategic interventions that are documented and carried out over a specified timeline, student success is expected to increase. If success does not occur at a particular tier, the student is moved to the next, more intensified tier until either success is achieved or the student reaches the last tier: referral for special education services.

- *IEP meeting*—The IEP meeting is similar from child to child. See page 15 for a simplified diagram of the process that occurs when a

Process for Planning an Individualized Education Program for a Student with Disabilities

Response to Intervention (RtI)

The student has gone through the 3 RtI tiers, and a recommendation for special education services has been made. The parents are asked for consent to test the student.

IEP Meeting – Step 5

General education is always the goal and is considered per the student's data. Placement and site selection are decided per the IEP, thus ensuring FAPE and LRE.

IEP Meeting – Step 6

The schedule page is completed, related services are set, and number of hours in special education and general education settings are determined.

IEP Meeting – Step 1

Committee members are invited to the IEP (individualized education program) meeting: parents, general and special education teachers, diagnostician, assistant principal, experts, student, and relevant others (e.g., lawyer, advocate).

IEP Meeting – Step 4

An IEP is discussed and agreed upon (annually). Free Appropriate Public Education (FAPE), least restrictive environment (LRE), related services, and/or extended school year (ESY) may be discussed at this time.

IEP Meeting – Step 7

Based on data and the student's academic performance, the committee decides what kind of academic assessment the student will receive and on what level.

IEP Meeting – Step 2

Procedural safeguards are given to the parents and/or student usually at the beginning of a meeting. Doing this ensures notice, consent, right to an independent educational evaluation (IEE), and right to due process.

IEP Meeting – Step 3

Eligibility is established through a full individual evaluation (FIE, at least once every 3 years), and a disability is documented or not (DNQ—"does not qualify"). An IEE may be requested.

IEP Meeting – Step 8

The signature page is signed. If all invited members agree, the IEP is in effect. If not, a 10-day recess is set. Next would come mediation, then a hearing. A parent may unilaterally refuse special education services at any time. Parent consent is required at initial and 3-year IEP meetings.

child is referred for special education services, and the role of the IEP meeting in that process.

Special Education Placements

A student is placed in a classroom or other setting in order to receive the most appropriate special education services. A list of placements and the types of students they are designed for is below; the names of placements may differ from the names used in your school district, but the concept and characteristics of each type of placement are the same.

- *General education*—Students who are not receiving special education services.

- *Mainstream/inclusion*—Students who are receiving special education services but may have a "monitor-only" status, may be able to handle the general education curriculum with minimal modifications, or may use a content mastery classroom (CMC) as needed.

- *Resource*—Students may have one to four or more classes with a teacher who is special education certified. The classes are usually core classes and some electives, depending on the school district's ability to find teachers with appropriate certifications.

- *Behavior management classes*—Students who have been diagnosed as emotionally disturbed through a psychiatric report will be placed in a type of behavior management class. Core and elective classes may be taught in this placement, and social skills must be taught. Counseling may be given, depending on a student's IEP.

- *Partially self-contained*—Students who are deemed "educable" and may receive all core classes in a partially self-contained classroom focusing on a life skills curriculum. Electives will include physical education (PE) classes and sometimes other general education electives, with a possible vocational job–related course.

- *Life skills*—Students who are "low-functioning" and who learn mainly on a prekindergarten to first grade level. They will have PE or adaptive PE and may go to job sites. Students in a life skills placement learn to cook, perform self-care tasks, clean, and so on.

- *Severe and profound*—Students who are medically fragile, mentally fragile, or severely autistic. This classroom is usually staffed with one or two teachers, many teacher aides, and possibly state-appointed or private nurses.

- *Hospital/residential*—Students who have been placed in a mental/emotional hospital or ward, per a doctor's or the state's orders. Depending on their health insurance, students may stay as long as two weeks to a year.

- *Homebound*—Students who are medically fragile or pregnant may qualify for homebound services if a medical doctor states that they will be absent from school for at least four or more weeks. Homebound services can also be given to students in general education, if they too have a medical reason for being absent from school for four or more weeks. However, a general education homebound placement is processed through a general education designee, like a counselor or an assistant principal.

The Sites

The sites, schools, or buildings in which some special education classrooms are located are listed and described below.

- *Home campus/school*—The school that a student is zoned to attend.
- *Regional day school*—A public school for students who are deaf and, in some school districts, for students who are blind. This is a specially designed school for the deaf and blind, with a specially trained staff and a specially designed curriculum and equipment (such as Braille writers). The whole campus is set up to meet the needs of these students (for example, Braille signs are posted).
- *Transfer to another school for services*—Not all schools may have the special education placement that a child needs; hence, a transfer to another school is acceptable (e.g., a school that has a behavior management classroom). Transportation must be provided for students who attend a campus other than their home campus. This solution is decided at the IEP meeting and is paid for by the school district.
- *Alternative school*—A specially designed campus for academic classes or discipline.
- *State school*—Every state has a state school for the blind/visually impaired and a state school for the deaf, usually located in the capital city. These schools provide special services and equipment to students who are visually impaired or deaf. They also provide summer camps and parent courses, along with adult services until the age of 21.
- *Hospital/residential*—This site category is usually chosen as a mental health placement for students diagnosed with mental illness and includes nursing homes for students who are medically fragile.
- *Day home*—An educable student may be placed in a day home while attending a public school. The student lives with like individuals who learn to cook, work, and function as a family and who are supervised by a caregiver 24 hours a day.

- ***Home***—A potential placement site for students who are medically fragile or pregnant.

As you can see, special education is a huge responsibility for any administrator. Consult your campus and district gurus to learn more about how this special program is implemented in your school district.

■ ■ ■

Curriculum and instruction are not just about what a teacher does in the classroom. They are so much more and require your understanding of the kinds of curriculum and instruction and their implementation methods that are present on your campus. In addition to using this chapter as a guide, find out your district's expectations for curriculum and instructional leaders at the campus level. If you feel overwhelmed at first, remember to ask for guidance from your gurus while you are learning.

CHAPTER 2
Traditional and Nontraditional Instructional Settings

New school administrators have much to think about concerning students and instruction. The various types of instructional settings seen on campuses need to be objectively observed by all administrators, so that the instructional delivery modes and student success can be understood. School settings are where instruction takes place, and many school districts are making changes in these settings. Most districts still hold classes in traditional environments, where students come to school for seven hours a day and sit in classrooms learning about assorted subjects. However, because students have diverse needs and because differences in how students learn are now recognized, non-traditional instructional settings, such as e-schools and specialized campuses, are on the rise. Settings also differ according to educational levels and the types of communities served.

Traditional Instructional Settings

The most commonly discussed school settings that administrators lead are elementary, middle, and high schools. The communities that make up school districts are usually classified as urban, rural, or military-oriented, and they help shape the learning environment. The characteristics of these various settings are important for administrators to consider as they learn about how and why teachers and students succeed or fail. Each of these campus settings is described below, with highlights of what can be expected at each.

Educational Levels

Elementary Schools
An elementary environment is young, new, vibrant, colorful, noisy, and busy. The environment feels young and new mainly because this is the level at which the youngest students enter school for the first time. It is vibrant and colorful because most elementary teachers enjoy creating bulletin boards with cute decorations and displaying student work on them. These touches foster

students' desire to be in school and to learn. The noisiness and high energy are due to excellent teachers being confident in delivering instruction through application-based activities and the use of manipulatives. In many classrooms, learning centers and collaborative groupings generate a boisterous atmosphere and controlled chaos.

Characteristics unique to elementary schools are many. It is important for new administrators, especially those who have never worked on an elementary campus before, to know what is typical of teachers at this level. The following, although not absolutes, are common at the elementary level.

- *Come early and stay late*. Elementary teachers frequently come to work early and stay late. Oftentimes they work on weekends and holidays. A consensus of why elementary teachers work long hours on campus is that they are constantly striving to perfect their craft, which translates into providing their young students with more and varied opportunities to learn and succeed.

- *Collaborating and sharing.* Elementary teachers have a reputation for collaborating, sharing, and discussing ideas for lesson plans. They also share books, manipulatives, and other resources and plan together as a team working toward being successful in the classroom. That spirit of collaboration and sharing is often extended to their students, in the form of learning centers or collaborative groupings where students learn from their peers, as well as from the teacher.

- *Early childhood.* Many elementary campuses offer classes from pre-kindergarten (pre-K) or early childhood through the fifth grade. Some may serve only pre-K through second grade students, while other campuses, known as intermediate campuses, accommodate grades three through five. Depending on the school district, early childhood levels may be housed on their own campus, where only three- to five-year-olds are served. Once those students pass to kindergarten, they are placed on an elementary campus.

- *Self-contained classrooms.* In self-contained classrooms, one teacher presents all core subjects, such as English, science, math, and social studies. In some schools, self-contained classroom teachers may also deliver electives or special subjects, like fine arts and physical education. Usually, classrooms are self-contained from pre-K through fifth grade, but some campuses start team-teaching at grades four and five. The purpose of team teaching at the latter grade levels is to prepare students for middle school, where they will switch classrooms and teachers throughout the day.

- ***Sponsored clubs.*** Some elementary schools allow students to join academic organizations. As early as third grade, students may participate in the student council or other clubs, like the chess club or the art club. Teachers volunteer to sponsor a club, overseeing the students as they meet or practice. If these sponsors will be handling money through an instructional fund account, they will need to have professional development on how to legally collect and spend this money.

- ***The student population.*** Depending on a school district's needs and number of campuses, an elementary school's student population may be as small as 200 or as big as 1,000. The size of a student body varies because of the school's design and the programs that are assigned to the campus. Some elementary schools are magnets or house a special program for the entire district, and other campuses send their students there. For example, an elementary school may be an AVID (Advancement Via Individual Determination) or an IB (International Baccalaureate) campus, and students from around the school district would come to this campus to get instruction from specialized AVID and IB teachers. Also common are special education classrooms, such as behavior management classrooms. This type of classroom might be housed only at certain elementary campuses; therefore, students who are assigned to them would be bused to that campus, thereby increasing the student population at that school and decreasing the home school's student population.

- ***Number of teachers.*** The number of students at a school will determine the number of teachers. For example, there may be between 15 and 60 teachers, one principal, and either no assistant principal or up to three of them on a campus. Campuses with only a principal will have lead teachers who help the principal fulfill some of the administrative duties. Additionally, special programs assigned to campuses will affect the number of teachers and teacher aides.

Elementary campuses are exciting places to learn. The teachers have a reputation of longevity at the same campus, but they also tend to be young themselves and may be starting their own families. So expect that some elementary teachers will be absent from the classroom for extended periods of time when they take maternity leave.

Middle Schools

When we think about the descriptors of a middle school, one word usually comes to mind: hormones! Middle schools have students who are spirited, loud, fad-conscious, self-deprecating, and consistently busy. Greater student involvement in diverse extracurricular activities is encouraged through academic clubs, fine arts, and athletics.

For administrators, working at a middle school is more than just a day job. Because of athletics and fine arts, administrators will have more duties that require them to work in the evenings and on weekends, such as attending an event as the administrator in charge or ensuring that all doors are locked after a music event. The following are some of the typical characteristics of middle schools that affect the administrator's role:

- *Come early and stay late.* Middle school teachers seem to always be at the campus. Some are there for athletic practice well before school starts, while others stay late for play rehearsals. Some coach students or lead them in games and competitions on the weekends, and others work during the summer to prepare students for the upcoming year. Academics, athletics, fine arts, and career and technology education (CATE) courses give teachers a chance to coach and sponsor students in extracurricular activities and make their responsibilities add up to more than a 40-hour-a-week job.

- *Collaborating and sharing.* "Teams," "houses," "families," and "pods" are some names that are given to groups of middle school teachers who share a group of students. The students assigned to a team meet with the their team teachers for instruction in the core subjects, while courses that are geared toward fine arts, athletics, and other electives are delivered by other teachers. The team of teachers works together to create interdisciplinary lesson plans and instruction that incorporates all core subjects. During parent-teacher conferences, they meet the parents together, supporting each other and the student. Collaboration and sharing will extend to the classroom, as some teachers will create learning centers and opportunities for students to work in collaborative groups.

- *Grade levels.* Usually, grades six through eight are housed at the middle school level. Some school districts may have centers or campuses specifically catering to one or two grade levels. For example, a junior high school might include only eighth and ninth grades, while a seventh-grade center may be devoted solely to seventh graders. There are many thoughts and ideas about why this is done, but the most common reason given for separating grade levels is to allow groups of students to mature and work with like peers without the pressure of older students shaping and influencing the campus.

- *Additional teacher duties.* Besides bus, lunchtime, and general be-fore- and after-school duties, teachers may also have responsibilities at assemblies, or after school and on weekends if they are sponsoring a club or a team.

- *Rigorous curriculum.* The curriculum for the middle grades, espe-cially the eighth grade, is much more rigorous than at earlier grade levels. In some districts, eighth graders can earn high school credits in fine arts, math (algebra), and some CATE courses (e.g., keyboarding). Such instruction parallels and prepares the students for high school classes, like U.S. history and English. The rigor of the curriculum is one reason why middle school teachers are certified in specific disci-plines and must be highly qualified.

- *Liability issues.* Because middle school students can participate in physical extracurricular activities, like football, gymnastics, dance, and others, some schools buy student and liability insurance to protect both the students and the school. Students and parents are asked to sign forms that provide information about their medical insurance, family doctor, and preferred hospital, as well as student health issues. Ad-ditionally, a student must have an annual physical exam by a medical doctor before being allowed to participate in a physical extracurricu-lar activity. Other schools avoid liability issues by offering intramural sports after school hours through a city sports league. Such teams may still use school facilities to practice, but the liability falls on the city league instead of the school district.

- *Drama and more drama.* Because of the hormonal changes they are experiencing, middle school students will sometimes display erratic, emotional, and impulsive behaviors. Students at this level are trying to discover what identity they want to project and how they can dress, look, and feel cool. They are also trying to learn how to handle daily situations with friends, heartthrobs, and adults. Consequently, they may come to school with a pleasant demeanor one day and a disagree-able one the next. Sometimes their demeanor changes by the hour, and the staff is challenged not only to instruct them each day and prepare them for the world beyond school but also to help them get through their mood swings and figure out what is socially acceptable behavior.

- *Preparing for graduation.* Due partly to special education guidelines and the need to discuss a student's transition from high school to adult life, many state education agencies have developed a personal gradu-ation plan (PGP) for middle school students. Usually during the sev-enth grade, each student consults with a counselor to develop a gradu-ation plan that highlights the student's goals after graduation (e.g., attend college or technical school, enlist in the military, or join the workforce). The counselor then works with the student and parents to find the best route for attaining those goals. For example, if a student is interested in learning how to work in a restaurant and owning one someday, then the counselor could suggest CATE courses that focus on both business and hospitality. The counselor would also point out which core classes and required electives are necessary for the student to graduate with a high school diploma. The PGP is a dynamic document, and each year the counselor, student, and parents review the plan, changing it as necessary. Students in special education follow a similar process, through a transition IEP (individualized education program). If the student is preparing to attend college or technical school or get a job, then his or her plan will look very similar to a general education student's PGP. For students who will need to be placed in a group home or some other kind of setting with 24-hour supervision after they graduate, input from a state's adult services agency would be a part of the conversation.

- *The student population.* Middle schools range from small to large, possibly housing 100 to 2,000 students. Middle schools that are magnet schools dedicated to special programs will have a student population that is especially diverse in talent, academics, and creativity.

- *Number of teachers.* The size of the teaching staff at a middle school can be anywhere from 15 to 200, for example, depending on the number of students on campus. More teachers may be assigned to a campus because of its particular needs. For example, fine arts, CATE, and athletic teachers are needed for their specialized fields. Additionally, if a school is very small, the principal might be its only administrator, but schools with a large student population might have as many as three assistant principals in addition to the principal.

Middle schools are always bustling with a constant stream of activities. Many middle school teachers have multiple teaching positions and therefore may be absent from their regular teaching position often. For example, athletic coaches will be absent on game days, while robotics teachers may be absent on competition days throughout the year. Thus, multiple substitute teachers will be a norm during certain parts of the year.

High Schools

High school campuses are large, busy, chaotic, spirited, and open seven days a week. They are the largest campuses in a school district, because all elementary and middle schools in a certain area of a city feed into a high school. They are busy and chaotic because many things are happening in different departments at once. They are spirited and open up to seven days a week because of extracurricular activities that create school pride. For administrators, this job is a 24-hour-a-day responsibility, and the demands can be many and can differ daily. Other characteristics of high schools that affect administrators include the following:

- *Come early and stay late.* Because of the many duties that high school teachers have, coming early and staying late are nearly required. Also, during specific times of the school year, teachers may need to come early, stay late, and work on weekends to meet deadlines and to assist students who are performing or playing in competitions.

- *Collaborating and sharing.* Every campus has numerous committees, and many of those on high school campuses have the same focus that their counterparts in elementary and middle schools do: campus improvement, safety/crisis, grade-level teams, social clubs, testing and assessment, curriculum, and parent-teacher association/organization. In addition, high schools have committees that focus on graduation; attendance and credit recovery; homecoming and prom; December, May, and August graduations; and discipline. Teachers on these committees are constantly collaborating and sharing with each other throughout the school year.

- *Grade levels.* Typical high schools serve students in grades nine through twelve. In some districts, high schools are divided into special campuses that house only certain grades, like a ninth- and tenth-grade center and an eleventh- and twelfth-grade center. As with the middle grades, the thought behind grouping particular grade-level students together is to increase their academic and emotional success.

- *Additional teacher duties.* Teachers are very busy at the high school level. Depending on what extracurricular-related duties they have (like working with the dance team), high school teachers may hold more than one teaching position. Teachers who coach or work with students who compete may receive a stipend for doing so. Such responsibilities should not be a part of a teacher's instructional evaluation, but they should be included in evaluations that address professionalism, teamwork, and campus success.

- *Rigorous curriculum.* Rigor in the curriculum is expected at the high school level because teachers are preparing students for life after graduation. In the eleventh and twelfth grades, students are able to earn both high school and college credit for certain courses through dual-credit or early-college programs. Both types of programs allow students to simultaneously enroll in high school and a local college, earning credits in college freshman and sophomore courses like English, social studies, science, math, physical education, and some electives (e.g., CATE) while also earning high school credits in the same areas. At these grade levels, students can also earn certification as cosmetologists, auto mechanics, or emergency medical technicians, for example. Teachers must be specially certified and highly qualified at the high school level, due to the advanced curriculum and the many specific disciplines taught.

- *Liability issues.* As with middle schools, student and liability insurance for high schools is bought to protect the students and the school, and parents must provide information about medical insurance, family doctor, student health issues, and preferred hospital to the educators on a campus. An annual physical exam must be completed by a medical doctor before a student can participate in a physical extracurricular activity. If a city sports league is used instead, the liability becomes the league's and not the school's.

- *School resource officers (SROs) and discipline.* The larger student populations at the high school level, as well as the age of the students, mean that the schools experience more discipline issues and penal code violations. Because high schools have higher rates of violations of the student code of conduct (SCOC)—specifically, violations related to drugs and weapons—SROs are permanent fixtures on many campuses because they are needed to complete arrests. School resource officers are peace officers, which means that their main function at a school is to prevent crime, enforce the law, and educate those on a campus about the law.

- *Technology.* Some school boards have established programs that encourage the use of technology in the classroom. One such program, started at many high schools, is the purchase of a laptop or tablet computer (e.g., iPad) for every incoming freshman. The staff and the students both participate in training to successfully use the new technology as a learning tool. After receiving the laptop or tablet, each freshman is responsible for its upkeep through the senior year of school. At that time, the district hands over ownership to the student as a graduation gift for use in college or at work. Some school districts start this program at kindergarten or in middle school. Others allow students to bring whatever technology they have to school to use in the learning process.

- *More diverse student body.* High school campuses generally have quite diverse student populations. Married students, pregnant students, students who work at night, and students who were dropouts and returned to school can all be found on a high school campus. This diversity prompts districts to offer nontraditional instructional settings to encourage nontraditional students to complete high school.

- *More personnel.* A registrar, a curriculum director, a student activities director, and an associate principal with assistant principals are all part of a high school. High school campuses have many more personnel than elementary and middle schools do, because high schools have more students and more requirements. For instance, depending on the number of students, two or more persons might handle attendance. A special education class for students with severe disabilities might have five teacher aides. A JROTC (Junior Reserve Officers' Training Corps) office might have a retired colonel, master sergeant, and first sergeant preparing cadets for military service. The registrar's office might have two or more persons diligently keeping up with graduation requirements, credit transfers, and assessment documentation to ensure that students graduate on time.

- *Graduation and beyond.* One of the main purposes of a high school is to prepare students for graduation and life after graduation. This is done by having them earn credits toward graduation in classes that get them ready for college, technical school, the military, or the workforce. As early as the middle grades, students discuss with their counselors the path they'd like to take to meet their life goals after graduation. Annual discussions about planning for life after graduation are encouraged, so that students are adequately prepared.

- *The student population.* The size of a high school is dependent on what the school board and the community desire. Small high schools may have 100 students, while others have more than 1,000. Some large cities have only one high school, with as many as 4,000 to 5,000 students, so that all student talent can be cultivated by the same specialized staff to take part in competitive sports, fine arts, and academic triathlons. Some smaller districts have one high school as well, but it may serve only 75 students, for example, because that is the total number of students in the city and surrounding area.

- *Number of teachers.* A high school's teaching staff may be as small as 15 and as large as 400. When the teaching staff is very large, the number of administrators is large as well, and usually the school is divided into houses, with one associate principal assigned as the principal for each house. A house would contain either one whole grade level or different grade levels with a specific number of students. Each associate principal may have several assistant principals assigned to the house to help with teacher evaluations, student discipline, and other duties. Furthermore, many high schools have schools within schools. For example, a high school campus could include a fine arts magnet school separate from the main high school. Before being accepted, students who want to attend the magnet school would have to apply, go through an interview process, audition or submit a portfolio of their work, write an essay, and provide references. Only those who go through the appropriate application process would be taught in the fine arts school, and all other students would attend the classes that are open to the general student population at the main high school.

High schools are complicated places, especially for an administrator who has never set foot on a high school campus. Although they are always busy, their workings can be impressive and they can run very smoothly, with a capable and readied administration at the helm. The expectation and demands at the high school level can seem a bit overwhelming, especially for the new school administrator, but being organized and flexible, delegating tasks, and collaborating with other educators will help you accomplish what is needed.

Types of Communities

If you pick up an educational journal or peruse the degree-seeking curriculum at a higher education campus, you may see the words "urban" and "rural" being used to denote differences between schools in urban and rural districts. For each of these settings, stereotypical assumptions are often made about the community, the schools, and how the students dress and behave. When you are seeking a job as an administrator in any given community, however, be sure that you leave your biases and preconceptions behind. Giving the people who live there a chance to show you what is important to them might dispel your prejudices and expectations. No setting is perfect, and each rural and urban school has its own assets and problems. Understanding those pluses and minuses may help you succeed in either setting.

Urban Schools

Urban schools have much to offer, mainly because of the vast amount of funding that is typically collected through taxes in urban districts. Unlike rural settings, urban environments encompass many homes and businesses that pay local and/or state taxes, a portion of which goes toward education. This money helps pay for the many resources usually available at urban schools. The following are some positive points about urban schools.

- Cities are divided into different communities, so urban schools essentially become community schools, catering to the students who live within or near the community.

- The body of students and teachers on a campus is usually quite diverse. The students may have different religions, upbringings, and ideas. More student associations that highlight such differences may be seen on the campus, such as political and religious clubs and clubs centered around sexual orientation.

- Urban campuses have more teachers and thus are able to offer a much richer curriculum. Classes in languages, such as French, Japanese, Spanish, Latin, and German, may be taught, along with an array of CATE courses in fields like law enforcement, aeronautics, and culinary arts.

- Newer and bigger facilities are ordinarily accessible in urban schools, as well as updated equipment and technology. Professional development and training are typically provided for teachers and students, respectively.

- Many opportunities and programs can be found within an urban school district, and students may request a transfer to a different school in order to participate in nontraditional instructional settings. Students sometimes have long bus rides to and from school in order to attend a special program on a specific campus, but each family can decide whether the benefits of the program outweigh this downside.

Some potential negative aspects of urban schools include these:

- The ratio of students to teachers is usually high and may be so overwhelming that disciplining students takes priority over teaching.

- Gang issues and serious SCOC and penal violations may occur more frequently than on a rural campus.

- Urban parents may work long hours on their jobs and thus may be less available to help their children with schoolwork and attend school events.

- Some parents in urban settings may be more apt to bring a lawyer to school-related meetings, just because they can or because they feel helpless. Both the parents and the students may feel that they can skip the chain of command and "tell on you" to the district superintendent. However, these behaviors may be seen in rural communities too.

With their abundance of courses, educators, and facilities, many urban schools are very successful in helping students achieve academically, with high rates of high school graduates and of students who go on to attend and graduate from four-year colleges. Moreover, participating in dual-credit and early-college programs is easier for many urban students, because they can either walk or take a city bus to a local college or university. The teachers are dedicated and enjoy living and teaching in urban settings, and the administrator who chooses to work in an urban environment is one who likes the busy and sometimes unpredictable nature of the schools.

Rural Schools

According to research studies, some common positives and successes of rural school settings are smaller student populations, higher test scores and graduation rates, and happier teachers (Barley and Beesley 2007; Cotton 1996; Raywid 1996; Viadero 2010; Wasley and Lear 2001). Teachers and other staff also tend to stay at rural schools longer than at any other type of school setting, due to higher job satisfaction and closer relationships with students, parents, and staff. Rural teachers are aware that working in an urban school district might be more lucrative, but many of them seem to be content with giving up the extra income in exchange for what they consider to be a better work environment.

Other positive facets of working at a rural school are that everyone knows everyone else, and the community helps its members, especially in times of crisis. This sense of community and closeness is a prominent cornerstone of rural communities. For instance, when a death occurs, it is the norm for the whole town to come together to help the family in any way feasible. Although individual families make up a town, the whole town itself—as a community—functions as a family.

The following are some positive characteristics of rural school districts:

- There is usually one campus per level (elementary, middle, and high school), and all three often are located on the same property. The school buildings tend to be relatively old and may be recognized by the state as historical structures. The district central office is sometimes found on the same property as well. If new schools are built, however, they might be placed at a different location within the community.

- Many rural schools have only one administrator per building; hence, there are no assistant principals. However, the administrator tends to be more involved in classroom instruction and student learning. The smaller student population and staff make it easier for an administrator to get to know everyone on a campus.

- The central office may be occupied by one superintendent with an assistant superintendent and possibly a director or two. The superintendent of a small rural school district is sometimes very knowledgeable and experienced regarding school finances and budgets, while other duties, such as curriculum oversight, are given to the assistant superintendent and directors. Several secretaries may be on staff to help with the paperwork.

- Individual teachers teach more subjects and, in some cases, hold more certifications for teaching different disciplines. They are more versatile and may teach at two levels throughout the day. For instance, a high school football coach may also teach middle school speech.

- Rural schools generally have lower student/teacher ratios, enabling teachers and other staff to get to know the students and parents better. Student and teacher success seems to be linked to lower student/teacher ratios, particularly in rural school settings.

- Many times, the teachers and other staff have grown up in the same rural community and now work for its school district. Therefore, the teachers understand the community and know how to get things done in the manner that is expected.

- Some instructional services may be contracted out through a cooperative, such as a special education co-op or a CATE co-op. Such arrangements allow several rural school districts to pay jointly for a service they all can access.

- The school district may be more apt than an urban district to use corporal punishment as a discipline tactic listed in the SCOC, and parents usually agree and support this measure.

Rural schools also have some potential negatives:

- Unless you live within the rural community, you may have to travel a long distance to work in the school district.

- The technology and textbooks may be outdated. Textbooks that are not current may be detrimental to student learning success, especially if a teacher relies only on the textbook and does not supplement the instruction with current information. Likewise, students are unable to become familiar with current computer programs if the school's technology is behind the times. The negative impact of outdated textbooks and technology on learning may become apparent when students are assessed through state testing and college entrance exams.

- Teachers are sometimes shared between campuses, so some teachers might not be available to students before or after school.

- Tax revenues are typically lower in rural areas, so the amount of funds a rural district has to work with can be substantially less than that in an urban district.

Like urban schools, rural schools can be quite successful in educating the children of their communities, and many students from rural communities achieve goals that are similar to those of their urban counterparts. Like urban teachers, rural teachers tend to be dedicated and happy in their position, and longevity is a norm. For administrators, the slower-paced and close-knit community becomes the attractive element.

Department of Defense Schools

Department of Defense (DOD) schools are much like rural schools: both are based in small, tight-knit communities that share a common background. The military has become quite family oriented, encouraging military parents to take part in their children's schooling and releasing personnel to attend school functions. Military families are usually very involved in their children's schools, mostly because they want to be but also because many post and base commanders allow time off for parent-teacher conferences and family activities.

DOD schools are well funded and have more amenities, such as gyms and indoor swimming pools, than some urban and rural schools do. More social workers may be available to help families cope with deployments, and ample military police and/or military probationary officers are available to visit schools often to work with students on probation. Additionally, JROTC programs are well funded, and post or base facilities are often used by JROTC cadets.

DOD schools generally follow the laws of the state in which they are located. The DOD schools on the military base at Fort Campbell, Kentucky, for example, follows Kentucky's state codes. Other military bases forgo DOD schools and partner with local school districts on education. In Texas, for instance, the Killeen Independent School District operates and controls many schools on the Fort Hood army post, with the support of the post. Although schools on military bases and posts are on federal land, they abide by state laws and school board policies, and they follow federal and state laws and guidelines for special programs.

Regardless of where DOD schools are, you will generally find that each has a dedicated staff that works hard to encourage students to do well, especially given the unique challenges that military dependent children face. The staff receives training on how to work with military families and children, and usually many of the staff are military retirees or military spouses.

Nontraditional Instructional Settings

To help students do well in school and graduate with a high school diploma, many school districts offer nontraditional classroom and campus settings—also referred to as alternative campuses for learning—for certain students. These schools and programs have qualifying requirements such as earning only five high school credits in a three-year period, dropping out of school, being pregnant, or simply being a particular age. Some school boards allow students at these alternative settings to be removed if they are truant or have behavior problems. The nontraditional instructional settings described below are not an exhaustive list but are the most common kinds of these schools and campuses.

Campuses for Overage Students

In some states, the education code allows students to attend high school until the age of 26. This stipulation has prompted school boards to create campuses that cater to overage students—that is, students who are 19 years old and older. These students may have been dropouts or may have lacked enough high school credits to graduate after their four years of high school. Campuses for overage students focus on helping them earn credits for obtaining a high school diploma and may be open 12 hours a day (e.g., 7 a.m.–7 p.m.), seven days a week. Often students come to the campus in four-hour blocks to work in an accelerated academic program. Usually these are self-paced programs that are computer based and fully online. Allowing students to attend school for only fours a day instead of a full day accommodates students who must work at a job or care for children part of the day.

Pregnancy Campuses

Some school districts offer separate campuses for both pregnant students and expectant fathers. These campuses deliver the same curriculum that the students' home campus does, in a judgment-free environment that focuses on both academics and parenting. Additionally, married students, with or without children, may have an opportunity to attend this campus.

E-schools

Electronic schools, or virtual schools, are becoming more prevalent in many states, catering to students who do not perform well in a traditional instructional setting. The e-school provides students a place to earn grades and credits in order to pass from one grade level to the next or to earn a high school diploma. An e-campus may be a better fit for students who are technologically savvy and proficient in understanding educational learning platforms, like Blackboard or Moodle.

Blended courses are also available at some e-campuses. In a blended course, a student spends half of the instructional time working online through a learning platform such as Blackboard, and the remaining half attending face-to-face classes with teachers and classmates. This type of learning is best for students who are able to work online but still need human interaction and confirmation.

Many schools charge a fee to attend the e-campus. In some cases, the fee is as high as $300 per credit. Such fees help pay for the learning platform, the creation or purchase of the curriculum, educational staff, technology support, and computers for student use. E-schools are usually housed on a campus, as a school within a school, and each usually has its own principal and staff.

Magnet, Charter, or Specialized Campuses

A campus with a specialized staff that hones in on one type of teaching could be called a magnet, a charter, or a specialized campus. (These terms are used synonymously in this section.) With the many special programs that school districts can offer, specialized campuses are becoming more and more common. Specialized campuses within your district might offer programs such as AVID (Advancement Via Individual Determination) or IB (International Baccalaureate), or they might be schools with names like Academy of Science, Academy of Literature and the Arts, Academy of the Fine Arts, Civic Leadership Academy, or Community Service Charter School.

To qualify to attend these types of campuses, a student must go through an extensive application process, which may include a series of interviews, submission of a written essay, a presentation of the essay or an audition to a panel of educators and peers, and recommendation letters from previous teachers. These campuses have rigorous curricula, and in many cases their students are prepared to attend Ivy League universities or military academies.

■ ■ ■

Find out what your school district offers in the way of traditional and non-traditional instructional settings, and guide your students toward the setting in which they are most likely to earn a high school diploma and prepare themselves to achieve their post–high school goals. If possible, gain experience at every educational level (elementary, middle, and high school) as a teacher or administrator. By doing so, you will learn about the many unique aspects of each type of campus.

CHAPTER 3

District Central Administration and Support Staff

At the district level, many staff members work hard to help each campus thrive and abide by federal, state, and local laws. These persons are dedicated to providing campuses with necessary employees, funds, and other resources. Understanding the functions of these district personnel and their offices will assist you in guiding your campus to success. This chapter presents an overview of personnel who can be found in a district's central office, along with descriptions of what their jobs entail.

Hierarchy of District Central Staff

The hierarchy of each school district will be distinctive, but the typical chain of command is organized as follows:

Superintendent

Deputy/associate/assistant superintendent

Area/regional superintendents

Executive directors and directors

Support staff at the district level

Principals

Assistant principals

Support staff at the campus level

The superintendent is the manager of the school district, the individual who works with the school board or board of trustees to hire and fire personnel, purchase and sell realty, create and approve policies and procedures, and do many other things that keep a school district running smoothly. The superintendent usually functions as the face of the school district, the person who meets and greets the community. The deputy, associate, or assistant superintendent is second in command and is usually viewed as the person who runs the school district. This person is designated to make the big decisions, especially on financial matters, and many in this position hold an MBA or an accounting degree. In some school districts, the person holding this position is known as the financial superintendent.

A school district may be divided into areas or regions, and a superintendent is assigned to oversee and lead the schools within each area. The number of schools in the district will determine the number of these area or regional superintendents. Each of these superintendents supervises and mentors the principals assigned to the area's schools, completes the principals' appraisals, and visits the campuses, performing walk-throughs and observations.

One area/regional superintendent may be assigned to the executive directors or the directors of the whole school district; however, in some school districts, the directors report directly to either the superintendent or the deputy/associate/assistant superintendent. The directors lead special programs, health services, nutrition services, transportation, maintenance, and custodial services. A district with many departments may have a multitude of directors. The directors are very knowledgeable about their particular areas of responsibility, and they may visit campuses that administer their programs.

Support staff members are found at both the district and campus levels. They function as administrators who support the departments and offices they are assigned to, but in official documents, such as their contracts, they are referred to as support staff. They may be akin to an assistant director in charge of a department, but to save money, some districts call them support staff, a position between a teacher and an administrator. Support staff usually are paid, not on an administrative pay scale, but on a teacher pay scale, plus stipends.

At the campus level, principals and assistant principals are the leaders. The principal is the face of the campus and may perform the meet-and-greet functions, while assistant principals take care of the daily matters, such as discipline, maintenance, oversight of special programs, and so on. The principal may also help with these daily functions. Both the principal and the assistant principals are responsible for the success of the campus, but the proverbial buck stops with the principal.

Hence, school district personnel are many and have direct links to the campuses within a district. In addition to the knowledge, experience, and information they can impart, they also have a lot of clout, so know who they are and learn what they can provide to your campus and how to obtain what you need from their offices.

District Central Administration

Several departments are commonly represented in school districts. The descriptions below will give you an idea of what to expect from these departments, although their functions may differ somewhat in your district. Each department may have its own director, each with his or her own leadership style, expectations, and understanding of how the department's budget works.

Assessments, Tests, Benchmarks

Given the number of periodic and annual assessments of students within a school district, a department of assessments, tests, and benchmarks is needed. This department is responsible for creating or obtaining assessment instruments to be administered throughout a school year in order to determine what knowledge the students have learned and retained. The results are then given to each campus principal, who shares the data with the teachers. The purpose of this department is to continually help campus personnel know how students learn, retain, and transfer knowledge.

Custodial Services

The custodians on your campus have been taught to perform their duties in accordance with federal, state, and local laws. Such laws address matters like how to use cleaning supplies, how to handle bodily fluids, and how to work on a campus full of children. Talk to your custodial staff to gain knowledge of what must be done on a campus and why they execute their duties as they do.

Curriculum

Many school districts have a director of curriculum or one or more superintendents over elementary and secondary curriculum. These individuals usually are tasked with ensuring that required state and national curricula are being taught precisely as prescribed and that students are prepared for benchmark and annual assessments. During the summer, this department may hire teachers to write curriculum, scope and sequence, lesson plans, or other kinds of tools for delivering instruction effectively.

Food Services

The food services department at the district level controls which food service personnel are assigned to each campus and how much money each campus is allotted. The director of this department must work not only with the funds generated by local taxes but also with state and federal money, which may include grants, especially if the district receives compensation for providing free and reduced-price meals. Each campus may have a food services lead or manager who directly answers to the district director of food services and the campus principal. The principal, however, does not have access to money that is allocated to food services.

Many rules are in place that cafeteria personnel must obey. For example, in order for a family to qualify for free and reduced-price lunches, an application with documentation (e.g., electric bill) must be presented to the cafeteria and administrative personnel. The purpose of the documentation is to prove that a family is in need of assistance and that it qualifies for this assistance according to federal guidelines. Additionally, students with food allergies must be identified so that the cafeteria workers may prepare food that is not harmful to them. The use of peanuts and peanut oil is sometimes banned altogether because some students may have severe allergies to them. Finally, regulations require that each student who buys a lunch through the cafeteria must receive a balanced meal of fruits, vegetables, protein, and whole grain. Students who do not have money in their account or do not bring a lunch may still receive a balanced meal, at the school district's discretion. Usually a peanut butter or cheese sandwich with milk is provided, along with a piece of fruit.

Class parties may fall under the jurisdiction of the cafeteria manager, per some state codes. For example, class parties may not include sweets to be shared, unless the party occurs after the last lunch on a campus. The last lunch period often ends at around two o'clock in the afternoon, a good time to schedule parties that involve snack or sweet items.

In many states, the education, health, or agricultural code will have rules spelled out for providing food services at schools. Appendix B contains examples of such codes from several states.

Health Services

The director of health services at the district level can be either a registered nurse or a general practice doctor. This director must be well versed not only in medical matters but also in both the education and health codes of the state. A nurse is assigned to each campus, and in some cases a nurse is shared among campuses. A nurse should be present on each campus at all times, but due to budget constraints and cuts, the nursing staff in many school districts has dwindled.

Nurses are essential staff members. When school registration is under way, parents must fill out a health form for each of their children, and those forms go to the nurse for review. The form is designed to alert the nurse and other personnel to any medical issues that a child may have, such as asthma, allergies, or cancer. The nurse will inform the educators who come in direct contact with the students who have medical issues. On many campuses, the nurse will create a list of affected students that includes suggestions on how to help them in case the need arises. For example, a suggestion in case a student has a seizure during class may be to ask another student to either call the office for help or seek the nurse for help. Additionally, the nurse will notify educators of special considerations to give students who have a medical need to use the restroom frequently.

For some students in special education who have medical concerns, especially those who are medically fragile or terminally ill, the state may assign and pay for a nurse to work only with a single student. Usually, if a child qualifies for a full-time nurse, three nurses will be assigned to the child within a 24-hour period. Your special education staff will get to know these nurses well, but you and your nurse also need to know who these nurses are, what their specific responsibilities are, and what they need to help the students they are assigned to.

The nurse and administrators are responsible for helping students stay healthy, which involves much more than providing balanced lunches and dispensing medications. While students are on campus, they are susceptible to injuries such as head traumas, cardiovascular traumas, concussions, and sexual assaults and to health threats such as accessible unprescribed drugs (e.g., steroids). There is no way that any administrator or educator can guarantee that students will be 100 percent safe from harm, but strategies can be put in place to reduce the risk of harm. Training all personnel on a campus about certain health issues that plague many students and adults may reduce risk or harm. For example, staff may be educated on how to recognize and respond to diabetes, obesity, bacterial meningitis, and child abuse. Such trainings may be a school board policy or a state mandate, so be sure that any required trainings are being delivered on your campus.

Take seriously any medical condition that a child has. Listen to the parents as they explain what their child needs, per their medical doctor, and provide what the child requires in order to be successful on your campus. In some cases, parents may give their permission for the nurse or you to speak to their doctor for confirmation. A doctor may determine that a student should be homebound for medical reasons, such as chemotherapy. Homebound school services must be given to any child whose doctor verifies that the child must miss school for four weeks or more. During this period, the nurse and you will need to work together with the parents and teachers to decide what is the best school schedule for the homebound student, since you have the authority to manipulate a student's school schedule to meet the child's needs. For example, if a student is stronger and more alert in the mornings, then scheduling the student's homebound services in the morning would be best. Additionally, if the student is strong enough to come to school on certain days but should be homebound on others, then a schedule can be flexible as long as the student is receiving an education.

Students in both general and special education are entitled to receive homebound services under Section 504 of the Rehabilitation Act of 1973 and under the Individuals with Disability Education Act (IDEA). If you do need to manipulate a student's schedule, then be sure to communicate with the attendance secretary on your campus to ensure that the student's attendance is recorded.

The health of teachers and other personnel is important too, and it can be helpful if you and the nurse know about the medical conditions of your staff. However, staff members may choose whether to let you know about their medical condition or not. That choice is their right, per HIPAA, the Health Insurance Portability and Accountability Act.

Hearing Officer

When a recommendation comes from an assistant principal for a student to be placed at an alternative school for discipline, a hearing officer must be present to be the impartial judge who will decide whether or not to uphold the recommendation. Depending on the procedures of your district, a campus-level hearing may be held, at which the principal is usually the hearing officer. This is typically followed by a district-level hearing, with the district hearing officer presiding. The hearing officer ultimately is given the authority to place a student in an alternative discipline setting for a determined number of days. More on the function of the hearing officer can be found in chapter 7, "Keeping the School Safe."

Human Resources

Hiring is the main job of the human resources department. When hiring people to work for a school district, the human resources department must ensure that certifications, background and criminal checks, licenses, and any other information about a prospective employee is sought, received, and deemed acceptable. Within the human resources department are suboffices that assist with employment-related tasks. These may include a substitute teacher request office, a fingerprint office, and an office that deals with highly qualified (HQ) teacher requirements, contracts, and certifications. Among other duties, this latter office mails letters to parents to inform them when an HQ teacher is not present in the classroom. Essentially, this office will help your district operate within the law.

Maintenance

Each district has a maintenance department that includes plumbers, electricians, carpenters, mechanics, horticulturists, and others. The main thing to keep in mind is that these personnel, like those who provide health and food services, have a primary boss or director at the district level. These employees will be assigned to your campus as the need arises.

Ombudsman

Investigations of complaints, as well as mediations and impartial data collection with an impartial recommendation on an issue are the job of the ombudsman. The ombudsman is like an investigator for the district, a person who seeks the facts about a situation and then makes a recommendation that is in the best interest of the school district. This person is the one to contact before contacting a lawyer.

Public Relations

As an administrator, you will want to get to know the public relations personnel, because as your teachers and students succeed and do outstanding things on a campus, you will want to brag about their accomplishments. The public relations office will be your point of contact to get your campus news out to the public. This office is also one that you may notify first when an unfortunate incident occurs on your campus. For example, if a student is harmed on your campus, this office may direct you to make no comments or to give a specific statement to the press and parents.

Law Enforcement

Many school districts have police officers present at all high schools and most middle and some elementary schools. Depending on its budget, a school district may have its own police department or may contract with the city police department or the county sheriff's office. The police officers assigned to a campus are usually referred to as school resource officers (SROs), who are specially trained to work with students, parents, and educators. They are peace officers, which means that they may carry a gun and other weapons, and they may make arrests. They ultimately follow the state penal code, and if a crime or violation of the code occurs in their presence, they will handle it and make an arrest. No confirmation to or consideration of the school administration is needed or warranted. These officers ultimately answer to the local police chief or sheriff, but they will coordinate with the school administration and inform the administration of arrests and other issues.

Some schools have both SROs and police officers present because of the size of a campus or the need to keep order. Police officers are specially trained to patrol the streets and to keep order of the general public. Still, some school districts have security officers, who do not require as much budgetary funding as police officers. Security officers are not peace officers, which means that they cannot carry a gun (unless certified to do so by their state) or make arrests except for breaches of the peace and felonies, for which every citizen has arrest powers. Security officers can help keep peace and order, but their authority is limited. SROs and security officers are discussed further in chapter 7.

Special Populations

The special populations department may be several departments in one, with a director for each special population represented within the district. Once you know what special populations are represented on your campus, you should make contact with this office to learn more about your responsibilities regarding them.

Technology

Technology is a huge department in many school districts, because it encompasses not only computer technicians and computers but much more. Many school districts are adopting BYOD (bring your own device) policies that allow students to bring their tablets, laptops, and smartphones to school. Such policies help students use technology for learning and retaining knowledge. Many teachers are now using tablets as a teaching tool, and students use them to learn and to produce work.

Additionally, e-schools and virtual schools are becoming more prevalent, because online learning is popular with nontraditional learners. School districts and many states have implemented pilot programs through which at least one school in a school district is virtual, which means that all learning takes place online. Technology and e-schools are discussed in more detail in chapter 2, "Traditional and Nontraditional Instructional Settings."

Transportation

At the district level, there may be one director of transportation for general education and another for special education. The reason for having two directors is that the director for general education is responsible for the entire district, while the director for special education works with confidential and sometimes frequent changes arising from decisions made in special education meetings. When a student has an annual special education or IEP meeting, transportation is discussed. If the meeting's committee agrees that the district must provide transportation for the student, the necessary paperwork is completed and submitted to the district transportation director for special education. The director and staff must maintain copies of the IEP paperwork at the district office in order to manage the different transportation needs of each student in special education. This paperwork also contains relevant addresses, phone numbers, and names of contacts. Furthermore, specialized vehicles may be needed for some students (e.g., lift buses for students with wheelchairs), and some bus drivers may need a bus aide to help keep student riders safe.

A smooth-functioning transportation department is extremely important to a school district, because provision of student transportation is complex, involving much more than scheduling bus pickups and drop-offs. If a district owns its own buses, it must have funds to ensure their maintenance, repair, fueling, insurance, and replacement, as well as the hiring of all personnel who will provide transportation services, including bus drivers and aides. Hence, this department is an expensive one. Because of the expense, some districts contract with school bus companies to pay an annual fee for the use of buses, and the fee covers all essentials in keeping the buses up and running.

■ ■ ■

Leading a campus is a big responsibility, and knowing that you must communicate with so many district personnel may seem intimidating. But keep in mind that working with district staff members can be easy and fun. Interactions should be collegial and focused on student and teacher success. Here are some ideas to help you have a great relationship with district personnel:

- Always be kind and courteous to district personnel, especially to the secretaries at district offices, whose work is often taken for granted. Get to know the names of all the staff members, and learn what their jobs entail.

- When district personnel visit your campus, be welcoming and transparent as you guide them through your school. A positive visit will enhance your position and strengthen future interactions. At the same time, perform your daily duties as you usually would, and know that you may be asked about how to improve upon them. One campus received a poor report after someone from the district's central office came on campus, and no one asked her to sign in or asked who she was and what her business was on the campus. Later, she questioned the adequacy of the school's check-in policies, which prompted the principal and assistant principals to institute a system requiring everyone to check in and out when entering and leaving the campus.

- Abide by the district personnel's requests and procedures. In other words, if you are asked to send paperwork on curriculum to the secretary, and not to the director of curriculum, then follow this procedure.

If you are to copy the secretary on each e-mail you send the director, then do so. Complying with such requests and procedures will bolster your relationship with district personnel. Remember, just as your own campus has established procedures, the district has ways of doing things that you are expected to follow.

- Invite district personnel to your campus for a breakfast or luncheon to orient them to your campus and staff, to say thank-you, or just to show appreciation throughout the school year. Sending thank-you notes with gifts that bear the school's name is always a great idea.

- Support district staff when they are on your campus. For example, if a student exhibits a discipline problem during their visit, then generate a discipline referral just as you would when handling a similar problem for one of your teachers, and with the same conviction.

- Money is allotted to these various departments, usually at the district level. You may find that money is allotted to fund these departments on your campus, but most likely you will not be able to touch it. Requests for more money probably will not be granted, but showing detailed documentation of the need for, say, an additional teacher aide might just get you what you ask for.

Be creative in coming up with ideas you and your staff can implement to ensure a positive relationship with the district central administration. Seek information from your school district on its hierarchy and organization and how you fit into it. Discover how to successfully maneuver throughout the district, creating collegial friendships and leaving no doubts about your leadership.

Leading through
Data-Driven Decisions

■ ■ ■

CHAPTER 4

Accountability of Administrators, Teachers, Students, and Parents

What is the meaning of accountability? To be accountable is to be responsible for something that has been assigned to you or left in your care or that you have volunteered to do. Being accountable also means accepting responsibility for your actions. For educators, this responsibility translates into giving students multiple opportunities to succeed in academics, behavior, and civility. Educators, therefore, must be accountable, or responsible, for everything they do, from providing students with learning tools to securing the campus or carrying out playground or football duty. Not only are educators accountable for students' progress in school, but students and parents are accountable as well. They must all work together to ensure that everyone takes responsibility for his or her part in educating students.

Although this chapter focuses on four specific populations (administrators, teachers, students, and parents), it is crucial for the campus administrator to recognize that all individuals who set foot on a campus are accountable for their actions. These include secretaries, substitute teachers, parent and community volunteers, nurses, counselors, cafeteria personnel, and so on. Everyone's efforts contribute to the successes on a campus.

Administrator Accountability

The chain of command on a campus always ends with the principal, but assistant principals are responsible for those duties assigned by the principal, so accountability for what occurs on a campus ultimately rests with the administration. Having so much trust given to you by your superintendent and school board may feel somewhat overwhelming and arduous at times, but if you remember the following tips, you will withstand the inevitable challenges and difficulties that come your way.

Consult the Campus Report Card

Each campus and school district receives a report card annually from the state and from the US Department of Education that delineates the degree of its students' success. The campus report card is full of data that should be shared with teachers, students, and parents. As the lead administrator, the principal must explain to them what these data mean, how to read and interpret them, and how to apply this information to improve teaching and learning. Much of an administrator's data-driven decision making will be determined by the data summarized in this report card, and the campus improvement team that establishes a campus's goals and objectives for the school year will also rely on these data.

Share the Responsibility

Many of the teachers on your campus will be willing to take on extra responsibilities to help the campus flourish. They will rise as leaders, if given the opportunity. You cannot singlehandedly run a thriving school, so accountability for certain duties and tasks on a campus must be shared. For example, some teachers will want to lead teams and committees, attend meetings in your place, work with you on a campus plan of action, or help write curriculum. Foster a spirit of collaboration, and allow your teachers to share in the responsibilities. In turn, be sure to share the glory of your school's accomplishments with everyone who has had a part in them. When everyone contributes to the campus's well-being, everyone should also share the kudos.

Conversely, when things don't go well on your campus, you, as the administrator, will receive much of the blame, even if collaboration was what caused an unfortunate outcome. Never forget that glory is shared, and blame is not.

Duties Can Be Fun

Discover ways to enjoy your administrative duties, because as you perform them, you are observable to students, educators, parents, and community members. In the course of your day, you'll have perfect opportunities to meet the people on your campus, to identify faces, and to strike up conversations with students. Parents appreciate seeing you on duty, because it shows that you care and that you are approachable. Teachers appreciate seeing you on duty, because it shows them that they are not alone. Students appreciate seeing you on duty, because they will feel safer and will be more apt to come to you with a request or a problem. Overall, being on duty is a positive aspect of your job.

Turn Confrontations into Positives

Many administrators, whether new or seasoned, are afraid of confrontation. Confrontation can be messy, but going through a necessary confrontation with another person can end positively, and the confrontation itself can be viewed as a positive. Because you are an administrator, conflict will find you. Learning how to handle conflict and work through tough situations is key to leading. Also, the teachers, students, parents, and everyone else who is invested in your school will look to you to see how you handle difficult situations. The following suggestions may assist you in dealing with conflicts and confrontations.

- *Conflict is a part of the job.* With so many different personalities on a campus, it is virtually inevitable that conflict will occur. As the administrator, keep in mind that conflict can be avoided if persons on a campus communicate specifically, frankly, honestly, concisely, and neutrally. Unfortunately, misunderstandings can arise from a person's perception of what has been conveyed through an email, a newsletter, a progress report card, a voicemail message, and so on. Therefore, it is wise to review with your staff how to compose messages and documents—by getting to the point, saying what needs to be said, and leaving no room for a misunderstanding. Educators should relay only facts and not emotions in all communication, and should support those facts with data and concrete evidence (discipline investigation, objective observations, etc.). Remind all staff that what is written and sometimes what is stated verbally can be used against them, and that concise language is best. For example, courts have subpoenaed educator emails and voice messages to discover exactly what has been communicated between persons and to determine the intent of communications, based on the language used.

- *Talk and work through the conflict.* Talking and working through conflict face-to-face can straighten out most misunderstandings and misperceptions. Having direct conversations and laying out all concerns truthfully and candidly will lead to a better understanding by all parties of the intended meaning of a communication. From these talks, better future communications can be developed because you will learn how to use specific language to get your point across.

- *Stand up to conflict.* Never run away from conflict, because eventually it will catch up with you. One of the worst things you can do as an administrator is to allow conflict to go unaddressed. Administrators are seen as leaders of a campus; hence, people will look to you to mediate and solve conflict. If you choose to run away from this duty, you may be perceived as weak and unable to take a stand. If you are one of the parties in a conflict, then be sure that you follow district policies and procedures when addressing the conflict and that you consider each element of the situation. Additionally, do not set a precedent by deciding not to enforce a policy in one instance, such as the student dress code, because some are likely to complain that you are "choosing favorites" or are enforcing the rules and policies only with those who don't ingratiate themselves to you.

- ***Don't give in just to avoid conflict.*** Finally, do not acquiesce out of fear or uncertainty. Have confidence in yourself as an administrator who is very familiar with the codes, policies, and procedures of the campus and the school district and enforces them according to school board policy. Additionally, show your confidence in knowing and upholding both state and federal laws and aligning them to the needs of the students. If you do not know how to address a parent's concern or answer a question, tell the parent that you will be more than happy to find out what is needed and that you will get back to him or her. Be sure to follow up with the parent so that additional conflict does not arise from lack of communication. Also, if a parent threatens you because of a perceived conflict, calmly remind the parent of the expectations of all persons who enter the campus; profanity and disorderly conduct will not be allowed. If the parent continues, then let him or her know that the police will be contacted if the behavior does not cease. Then call the police, and take care that everyone around you is safe and secure. The police will issue a citation or ticket as needed.

Addressing conflict becomes easier with practice, especially since conflict sometimes leads to better and stronger relationships with others. Additionally, working through conflict may demonstrate that you, as an administrator, can be trusted to be fair to each individual on a campus.

The Kids Are All Right, and So Are You

The prospect of being responsible for so many students, with so many different needs, may be a bit scary for a new administrator. One assistant principal had worked with high school students for years, and her first position as a principal was at an elementary campus. She was afraid that she would not be able to relate to the students or their parents. But she soon found out that kids are kids and can be fun to work with at any academic level. Another person was promoted to an assistant principalship at the high school level after teaching fifth- and sixth-grade students for many years. He found that the older students were easier to talk with, and he liked having more "grown-up" conversations with them. Rest assured that the students on your campus will grow on you, and you will come to enjoy the level at which you are working.

At various points, students will vie to push your buttons, just to see whether they can upset or irritate you. But the number one rule to learn right away is, *Let everything roll off your back, and never take anything personally.* Remember this in every interaction you have with students, parents, and other educators. You may be called every name in the book; you may even be hit, have things thrown at you, or be verbally threatened. This sort of reaction has little or nothing to do with you as a person, but everything to do with you as an administrator, a person in a position of authority. Unfortunately, some students (and parents too) believe they have to yell and scream to get their ideas across. Although it is not your job to take abuse, sometimes allowing a person to vent can help you both get to the bottom of a situation and can strengthen the perception of you as a caring and compassionate person throughout the school community. So grow some thick skin and a strong backbone, because as an administrator, you will need them.

Support the Teachers—and Everyone Else—on Your Campus

Neila Connors wrote a book with a title that expresses the perfect administrator's philosophy. It's succinct and easy to remember: *If You Don't Feed the Teachers, They Eat the Students!* This one sentence says it all, because if you don't take care of the teachers (and everyone else) on your campus, they may not feel motivated or supported enough to help students perform to their potential.

The first thing to remember when working with teachers is that all of them have at least a bachelor's degree, and many may have a master's degree and a doctorate. In short, they are educated professionals who have been taught how to teach. Second, teachers are adults and should be considered as such. They do not need to have their hands held, to be threatened, or to be ignored. They don't need to be controlled like children who must ask permission for everything. Of course, for accountability's sake, certain items, such as lesson plans, must be submitted for approval, and some activities, like field trips, may need your permission before they are ventured. Overall, though, regarding teachers as colleagues and not as inferiors is essential. The atmosphere on your campus starts at the top—with you, as the administrator. All you have to do is treat teachers (and all other persons) with respect and collegiality, and they will respect one another. This is supporting your teachers, who will in turn support their students.

Additionally, everyone wants to be liked, especially new administrators, but in some cases, being liked by parents may seem more appealing than being liked by teachers. For example, when dealing with a difficult parent, especially one who threatens to go to the superintendent, an administrator may want the situation to end and confrontation to be averted. Such threats make administrators feel as if they are losing control of their campus, and they want to avoid having criticism reach the superintendent. Hence, an administrator may agree to the parent's demands, even if doing so places a teacher in an impossible position. For some administrators, it seems easier to back everyone but the teacher.

But backing your teachers yields a bigger payoff than not doing so. First, it is ethical and just to stand by those persons on a campus who help support you and the students. In order for teachers to feel as if they matter, as if they are professionals, and as if what they do counts, they must be valued. In return, they will work hard to ensure that students succeed, and they will back your efforts to accomplish this.

Remember, It's "We," Not "Me"

It can be pretty exhilarating when you earn an administrative position. Because you have accomplished a goal you worked hard for, you may feel as if your time has come and everyone should take notice. But remember where you came from. You were a teacher once, and you must always remember that campuses benefit when administrators work with teachers as a team, rather than excluding them from the decision-making process.

When speaking about the campus to others, refer to "our campus," "our accomplishments," and "our students." Say that "we are working toward our goals" and describe how "we are striving to succeed." When you use the words "we" and "our" when referring to your campus, your teachers will eventually do the same. Teachers need to hear that "together, we can make good things happen."

Get the teachers in the habit of working for the whole campus, and not just their classroom, grade level, or discipline. In everything they do—whether it's parent-teacher conferences, assigned duties, teaching, or chaperoning a school dance—teachers should be focused on student success. Only then will teachers describe what occurs on a campus by saying, "We did this," instead of something like "The ninth-grade teachers messed up again. Their kids didn't score well on the state tests."

Brag about Your Teachers

Sing the praises of your teachers, especially to parents, community members, and other educators. Be specific in what you highlight: that one engaging lesson, the play-off game, the student council presentation. Invite the media to come see what your teachers and kids are achieving.

Urge the teachers to talk about their accomplishments too. If they are too shy or modest to bring up the remarkable things they and their students are doing, then ask them to tell you so that you can spread the word. Encourage the students, parents, community members, and other educators to brag about your extraordinary teachers as well.

Remember to honor teachers who go above and beyond the call of duty.

Recognize those who are willing to give extra time to the school, and validate their efforts. Again, sharing the glory and bragging about these teachers will do more to help a campus family become cohesive than almost anything else.

Expect Teachers to Be Unique

All teachers are unique. They have different strengths and weaknesses, different gifts, and different expectations for themselves as professionals. Most, if not all, teachers will want to be a part of the campus "family," but when the time comes for teachers to volunteer to sponsor a student club/organization or attend a PTA/PTO meeting, for example, don't expect every teacher to participate. Some of your staff will attend every event, others will come to some, and a few won't participate in anything. Don't fault anyone for their choices, because extracurricular activities will be covered one way or another (usually parents will help out too). The teachers know their strengths and weaknesses and will volunteer for the activities they feel comfortable participating in.

Don't Be Afraid to . . .

Don't be afraid to fail. Many people will expect you to fail as a new administrator on a campus, not because of who you are personally, but because you are in a coveted position. People who interviewed for your position, who aspire to your position, or who think they know all about you from rumors they've heard may even hope that you fail. Put such sentiments aside, and prove these doubters wrong. Through your stamina, consistency, fairness, and knowledge, show that you belong on the campus as its administrator. You will make mistakes, as everyone does; and when you do make a mistake, admit it and fix it. Allow the teachers and everyone else to know that you are human and that not everything you do will be perfect, but show them that you will learn from your mistakes.

Don't be afraid to stand up for your teachers. Your teachers expect to be supported by you, especially if they feel that they are skillful teachers. When parents do not follow the campus's chain of command and instead come directly to you before consulting a teacher, they will expect you to take their side and to punish the teacher. One principal who allowed parents to come straight to him with any complaint about a teacher always took the parents' word as truth without ever asking the teacher for her or his perspective on the situation. This policy obviously made working for this principal very difficult for teachers, and transfer requests under his administration were nearly 75 percent every year. Don't be this kind of an administrator. Don't allow parents to jump the chain of command, ignoring the professional courtesy that should be given to the teacher. Remind the parents to talk with the teacher first, giving that teacher an opportunity to hear about their concern and have time to respond. Intervene only when the teacher requests your assistance or if the situation warrants your attention (for example, a parent makes threats). If it should come to pass that the teacher is wrong, then apologize to the parent for *your* mistake (not the teacher's) and correct it immediately. Then have the teacher correct his or her mistake.

Don't be afraid to start traditions, even if the teachers balk initially. For example, one principal started a round-robin sing-along at an assembly, to follow a holiday-season program performed by students. At the end of the program, the performers and the audience were asked to sing together. The teachers thought that a sing-along at an urban middle school was ridiculous, but the principal insisted, and the assembly turned out to be the most enjoyable and productive one that year for both the students and the teachers. Expect teachers to be doubtful about some of your ideas, but give them a chance to tell you why they are hesitant and to offer possible alternatives. Conversely, some teachers may propose an idea that seems unfeasible to you, but allow them to try it out, because—to your surprise—it just might work.

Teacher Accountability

Teachers are familiar with their responsibilities and their accountability for fostering student success. They understand what campus accountability means too, but sometimes it will be necessary to clearly make your expectations known. For example, if you are a new administrator on a campus or if a teacher is new on the campus, you must both become familiar with what each of you is accountable for.

The first thing to find out about as an administrator is which grades and subjects each teacher is accountable for. This is very important because the report cards for both the campus and the school district will show the classrooms whose students are succeeding and the classrooms where improvement is needed. Furthermore, certain grade levels and subjects are referred to as the "accountability grades" and "accountability subjects"; students are tested at these grade levels and on these subject areas at the state level, and their scores become a part of the school and district report cards. Knowing which teacher teaches which subject or grade level will help you be aware of which teachers may be a bit more stressed in accomplishing their job, because they are teaching in these accountability areas. Their students' scores are made public and are judged by everyone who sees them, including parents, community members, and other educators. Support these teachers by providing the resources they need (as you would with all of your teachers), and pay close attention to how the students in these classrooms are doing. Many times you will find your gurus and master teachers among this group.

The second thing to keep in mind is that it will take some time for teachers to warm up to you and trust that they will be fairly appraised as accountable educators under your leadership. As a new administrator on a campus—regardless of whether you are a new assistant principal, vice principal, or principal—you can bet on going through at least a semester before teachers feel comfortable with you and the way you lead. During that semester it is imperative that you do the following:

- *Be as genuine as possible.* Teachers will know if you are being real or fake. They will question other people to get to know a lot about you, so be honest, transparent, and frank. Some teachers may even try to push your buttons or resist your leadership. If this occurs, have a heart-to-heart with the teacher and emphasize that collegiality will always work better than friction.

- *Say what you mean, and do what you say.* There is no time for beating around the bush or trying to be so diplomatic with your words that the meaning is lost. If you need to say something, then say it. Be frank, yet respectful. Be honest, yet tactful. Be helpful, courteous, and caring, and your teachers will respond in kind. Also, model what you need the teachers to do, and do what you expect others to do. For example, if you have asked teachers to lock their classroom doors and turn off the lights before they leave for home, then you must do the same.

- *Get to know the teachers on both a personal and a professional level.* Just as the teachers are trying to get to know you, you need to get to know them. Find out what their likes and dislikes are, whether they have children, if they are attending graduate school, and so on. Then use this new knowledge in conversations when getting acquainted. Let them know that you care and that you want them to be successful. Getting to know your teachers will also help create a familial atmosphere.

- *Visit classrooms often.* Visiting classrooms is one way you can get to know the teachers and students. You will see how teachers deliver instruction, how students respond to the instruction, whether the teachers and students have a good rapport, and whether learning is really occurring. Teachers need to expect that you will come to observe or walk through their classrooms anytime, without notice in most cases. They also need to believe that you are frequently observing their classrooms so that you can be fair when evaluating their teaching.

- *If you expect it, then follow up on it.* If you assign teachers to bus duty each morning from 7:30 to 8:00 a.m., for example, then follow up with the teachers to make sure they are performing this duty at the designated time. If they are not doing so, or if they are often late, make it clear to them that being on duty is important for student safety and that the ramifications could be dire if an accident occurred when they were not at their post. In addition, demonstrate the significance of such obligations by performing duty shifts yourself. If you are willing to assign duties or tasks to teachers, then you must be willing to carry them out yourself as well.

- *"Help me help you."* Teachers may need to be taught and reminded that when they seek your assistance, you will need to know all of the facts before you attempt to resolve a situation. For example, if a parent complains to you about a teacher's methods, you will relay the complaint and allegation to the teacher and ask the teacher for her or his view of the situation. You must find out all the facts, no matter how offensive or damaging they may be, so that you can perform your job effectively and fairly with both the teachers and the parents. If the facts are not all known or are unclear, then you risk being accused of not knowing what is going on right under your nose, as well as appearing foolish or unprepared to parents or outsiders. So teach your teachers to help you help them as you perform your job.

Professional Development

Teachers can also learn about accountability through professional development. Professional development has a significant role in an educator's career, and teachers are required to attend a certain amount of hours of classes each year to enhance their skills. The key aspects of professional development are these:

- Professional development should be aligned with what the teachers are teaching or what they need to know in order to perform their job better.

- It shouldn't be a waste of time, and the concepts covered should be implemented in the classroom immediately after the training and throughout the year.

- The success of both the teachers and the students should increase after teachers receive professional development, and that success should be evident in the teachers' evaluations and the students' standardized test scores, or the like.

- The teachers and the school administration, instead of those at the district or state level, should collaborate on choosing all professional development at the campus level. They know best what is needed to foster success on their campus.

Teacher Assistants

Teacher assistants (TAs) are valuable personnel who can contribute to the success of teachers, students, and the campus as a whole. They should be treated as professionals and, like teachers, should be told clearly what is expected of them and how to fulfill those expectations. In many school districts, TAs are trained to execute certain assignments. For example, a level 1 TA usually can assist in any classroom or office, doing tasks such as tutoring, grading, filing, or answering phones. A level 2 TA may be assigned to particular classrooms and/or students, helping the students acquire the curricular concepts and objectives. For a more specialized classroom, such as a special education one focused on life skills or behavior management, a level 3 TA may be trained to work with students with specific disabilities. Their professional development may include courses on crisis prevention and intervention or on how to use an array of equipment, like DynaVox communication devices and Braille machines.

Student and Parent Accountability

Students and parents also are responsible for their actions and for helping students succeed in school. Student responsibilities include academics and behavior, and parental responsibilities are related to behavior and support. Both students and parents need clear guidelines on what is expected when they are on campus and when they are interacting with others.

The ultimate responsibility students have at school is to take advantage of all opportunities to succeed academically, behaviorally, and emotionally. Another essential student responsibility is to help keep the learning environment free of disruptions. Parents in turn are expected to support the educators on a campus and to reinforce campus rules and policies so that students are motivated to follow them. Additionally, when parents are supportive partners of educators, the probability of success increases for both the students and the teachers.

Many schools and school districts have Parent/Student Handbooks and Student Codes of Conduct (SCOC). In each, rules, policies, procedures, instructions, and expectations are outlined. Be sure that the teachers and all administrators on your campus are aware of these handbooks and of other materials being sent home to parents. It is good practice to have teachers review and teach from these handbooks during the first week of school and as needed throughout the year. This helps everyone remember the expectations of the school.

Overall, keeping both students and parents informed will encourage them to work toward being accountable. Some reminders for all administrators to convey to parents follow.

Give Educators the Benefit of the Doubt

Some parents will ask their children how their day went, and the children will relay their perception. Parents may misunderstand that perception or blow it out of proportion, leading them to ask the administrator to punish a teacher. In such situations, you must ask the parents to allow for due process—giving all parties in the situation, including the teacher, a chance to tell their side of the story—before coming to a conclusion.

Never discount a parent's perception, however, no matter how ridiculous it may seem, and keep in mind that students report to their parents what is occurring on the campus, or at least the students' perception of it. Parents may relay this perception, sometimes with embellishment, to other parents and community members, until eventually it reaches the superintendent. Sometimes this viewpoint is glowing and positive, and sometimes it can be damaging and slanderous. Just remember that parents will talk, no matter what facts they do or do not have, so it becomes imperative that you provide students and parents with detailed information about all that is occurring and expected on your campus. Additionally, you must stress that giving others the benefit of the doubt and not jumping to conclusions will help build positive relationships between parents and educators.

Welcome Parent Involvement

Some schools are fortunate to have a great deal of parent involvement, and others do not have enough. There is no magical secret for getting parents involved at a school, but keeping them informed of events happening on a campus, like an open house, will encourage them to participate.

To gain parental support, some public schools have adopted a strategy used by some private schools. A contract is created between the school, the student, and the parents, listing the exact duties of each. For the parents, the duties might include working concessions at basketball games, providing baked goods for a fundraiser, or volunteering as a class parent. When parents fulfill their part of the contract, oftentimes the success of their children in school is evident. When parents don't fulfill a contract, the school might add different kinds of duties that are more attainable or might enforce a consequence, such as not allowing the parents' children to participate in class parties.

Be Transparent

Students and parents seek to know the expectations of a campus, so provide them verbally and in writing. Together with the teachers, make a list of expectations to send home throughout the school year. For example, parents need to know the expectations for dropping off and picking up their child, visiting the school and classrooms, sending money to school, sending medication to school, following the chain of command, and so on. Things will run so much more smoothly when students and parents know what to do.

Keep the Peace

Sometimes parents are very impassioned when making a demand. They may verbally abuse a teacher or an administrator, or they may display other behaviors that put educators at risk. At such times, you may need to remind the parents that they cannot interrupt the learning environment or disturb the peace. Additionally, reminding them that a citation or an arrest could be imminent may help diffuse the situation. Never be afraid to call for help, and always seek to keep those in the vicinity safe from harm, including yourself.

Try to Resolve Confrontations with Parents

Sometimes an angry parent may confront you about something involving their child, such as a suspension. As stated earlier, confrontation can be difficult, but do seek a positive outcome when confronted by difficult or angry parents. Not all confrontations will end in a positive outcome, however, especially if you are dealing with something like a student's arrest for a crime committed on campus. Nevertheless, difficult confrontations often lead to positive outcomes if the following suggestions are adhered to.

1. ***Talk.*** Each person should have the opportunity to state her or his perception of the issue at hand and the cause of the conflict. Allowing a parent to voice his or her understanding of a situation, without interruption, will help you find and present solutions, when the time comes. While a parent is voicing these perceptions, be sure to document what is being said. After the parent has had a chance to say all that is on his or her mind, then it is your turn to express your understanding of the situation. You should also remind the parent of the campus goals and objectives, of the Student Code of Conduct, or of any other mandate, policy, code, or law that you must follow, as appropriate to the situation.

2. ***Listen actively.*** As you actively listen while the parent speaks and document what is being said, also look at the parent. Looking at the person speaking shows that you are listening, that you care, and that you are willing to work with him or her. When it is your turn to speak,

repeat back to the parent what was stated and what you heard as the source of conflict. While you speak, continue to look at the parent and any others who may be at the meeting. Then express your view of the situation. Be honest and frank, but tactful. Don't beat around the bush, especially if you need a parent to stop doing something or to follow the rules. For example, if a father refuses to sign in at the front office before going to his son's classroom, you will need to tell him that his failure to sign in may lead to a trespassing citation.

3. *Seek a solution.* You and the parent should each state what solutions you desire, and you can then state what compromises, if any, can be made to implement a particular solution. For example, the solution a mother may want is for you not to suspend her daughter from school for three days. You may choose to compromise or not, depending on what data you have gathered from your investigation of the incident and what other disciplinary actions have been taken with this student in the past. Nevertheless, the solution should align with the SCOC and with school and district policies.

4. *Collaborate on making a pact or contract.* At this point in the process, a collaborative effort toward a solution should be tried. The agreed-upon solution may be to enter into a parental involvement contract or some other kind of parental pact. The contract or pact should be both verbalized and written, and all parties concerned should sign the written document. You will keep a copy, and you will give a copy to the parent.

5. *Revisit and evaluate.* Revisit the pact or contract at a predetermined date and time, evaluate the progress made, and change or dismiss the pact or contract as the situation warrants. The action taken should depend on documentation supporting the change or dismissal of the pact or contract, and this step should also be an opportunity for you and the parent to voice any additional concerns. Ultimately, the decision of whether to continue the contract should be based on the best interest of the students on your campus.

Again, some confrontational situations will not lend themselves to the above prescription. In cases where there can be no compromise, such as the arrest of a student for a crime committed, no pact or contract would be developed, because you will not be able to negotiate with the parent. You may, however, talk with and listen to the parent and provide the parent with information on what the next step for the student may be.

■ ■ ■

Accountability ultimately applies to every person who sets foot on your campus. It becomes your responsibility to ensure that everyone abides by all of the expectations, rules, policies, and procedures of your campus, so be sure that everyone is aware of them.

CHAPTER 5

Finance and Budgets

Finance and budgets can be intimidating concepts for new administrators, particularly those who have had little previous experience with developing and overseeing budgets. This chapter provides an overview of the most important aspects of a school's money matters that you must understand as an administrator, whether you are a new principal or a new assistant principal charged with managing the school's budget. Ultimately, you will learn on the job, by patiently and continuously working with your own campus budget. When spending the money that has been allotted to your campus, documenting and accounting for each penny spent will make handling your school's finances easier and will become second nature.

Find Your Focus

When you get the news that you have been hired as a school administrator, you may think, "Oh my gosh, I have arrived!" Well, you may have arrived, but you have much work to do before anyone perceives you as a viable, fair, and successful administrator. To gain those accolades in the area of finance and budgets, you must learn all you can about what it means to spend money legally and efficiently on behalf of your campus.

Ideally, your school district will provide briefings and professional development sessions on the federal, state, and local requirements regarding budget matters. You will be inundated with so much information that it probably won't all sink in at first. Plus, there are so many codes and functions at all three levels—federal, state, and local—that there is no way to remember all of them, even after many years of leading a campus. Furthermore, federal and state codes are established by legislatures and are constantly changing, so the best thing to do is to focus on the financial matters that are related to your campus, such as the kinds of monies allotted to each fund and for what purpose, and how much is being spent.

Nevertheless, you must understand the codes and functions that apply to you and your campus. When learning about them, an administrator will be given information, definitions, and directions on how to spend money per these regulations. It is the administrator's responsibility to keep up with what these regulations entail, so as not to be accused of spending money haphazardly and inefficiently. Often administrators will have one or two secretaries share the burden of understanding school finance and budgets, but it is ultimately the administrator who is responsible. Furthermore, when regulations are not followed, state educational departments have been known to audit schools and to rate them on how money is being spent and whether the spending aligns with the regulations. If the audit report finds anything other than what is legally allowed, then sanctions, loss of money, or possible loss of accreditation may result. Even though finance and budgets are a big part of an administrator's job, finding your focus and honing in on the purpose of school funds will help you spend your school's money according to the law.

Tips on Handling the Money

The approach you take to handling school funds will largely depend on the type of campus you are assigned to. If you are a new administrator on an established campus, look at the financial systems already in place and find out who has been keeping up with the money. Then, don't change the way things are currently being done, but instead continue what has been working well. If you are a new principal at a new campus that you will help open, then you must discover what has been successful at similar campuses and implement those practices. In either case, you will keep acquiring knowledge as you go along. Try not to be frustrated when you don't understand something. Instead, ask lots of questions, trust in at least one other person on campus to double-check your work, and learn from your mistakes.

Many administrators have managed their school's finances well because they have a good understanding of key areas of the budget that remain constant. For a positive and successful experience, familiarize yourself with the types of funds that commonly are part of a campus budget.

Types of School Funds

A fund is money allotted for a specific purpose, and usually one or two persons are responsible for keeping an account of the fund's income and expenditures. The following list describes funds typically allocated for various activities on a campus. This is not an exhaustive list, however, and some of these funds may have different names in your district.

General Fund

The general fund is the biggest fund, with the most money, and is used for everyone on a campus. It covers most routine expenses, like salaries, substitutes, utility bills, furniture, and copying and printing costs. Money in the general fund can be spent on almost anything but is usually reserved for big-ticket items.

Instructional Funds

Instructional funds come from the general fund and are meant for anything that deals with the instruction of all students on the campus. Teacher workroom supplies, computers, textbooks, and science lab materials are examples of what can be purchased. This fund is created and supplied by the district; therefore, it is to be spent for the good of all students, whether they are in general education or in any special program.

Activity Funds

Activity funds are one of the most liquid types of funds, because your teachers, other administrators, secretaries, and you may be adding money to and withdrawing money from these funds as the need arises. These are campus-generated funds, which means that money is collected and spent based on campus needs and in exchange for a product. For example, yearbook money is placed in an activity fund (called the campus activity fund in some districts); students are asked to pay for a yearbook, and then an order is placed based on the money collected. Another example is the purchase of T-shirts for a particular club. Students give their payment to the teacher, who turns the money in to the office. When the T-shirts are received, the bill is paid out of the fund (called the student activity fund in some districts), and the students are given their T-shirts. Hence, in both of these examples, the money is generated and spent at the campus level for purchases. Money can also be donated to this type of fund, and district paperwork will need to be completed and sent to the district office to prove that the donation was meant for the school and is ready to be spent from the activity fund.

For vending machines, districts may give principals the ability to sign contracts with approved vendors to place vending machines on a campus. Other districts have someone at the central office enter into the contracts. The profits from the vending machines may be put in a campus activity fund and spent on whatever the administration deems needed, like school supplies. Or the district may have control of the money, placing it in the district account and spending it for the benefit of the campus, such as purchasing new office equipment.

Usually a separate fund is set up for each activity or group, such as each grade level, each student club, the band, and the student council. The money in these funds is spent on items that promote student success, like classroom supplies, field trips, and book studies. Activity funds can also be spent on social activities, like class parties, homecoming, prom, school carnivals, and other school events. How money is spent depends on the needs and expectations of an activity or group. Activity funds are handled solely by the campus, within the limits the district sets. Make sure you know your district's rules and regulations regarding activity funds. Check with the district office if you have questions about procedures for collecting and disbursing money from these funds, because misappropriation or misuse of these funds may result in criminal charges.

Grants and Special Programs Funds

Grant monies and special programs funds are usually centrally located and disbursed from the school district's central office or grant office. This money is destined for the education of students who are in a special program, in addition to money that may be spent on these same students from the general or instructional fund. This money may be spent on anything that is needed for these students to be successful, like closed-circuit TVs for students who are visually impaired. Know what grants are assigned to your campus, because these monies can be spent only on the program designated by the grant. For example, grants for English-language learners (ELLs), talented and gifted (TAG) students, Title I, and special education pay only for services allotted for students in those programs. So, for example, grant money used to hire a teacher's aide for special education is a legitimate expenditure only if that aide works solely with special education students in special education settings. This means that the aide can't help in another classroom, unless the purpose is to assist students receiving special education services in that classroom. Likewise, the aide can't be pulled from a classroom to help out in the front office.

Average Daily Attendance Funds

States use student attendance—also known as average daily attendance (ADA)—as the basis for determining state funding of schools. The state projects the student attendance on your campus for the upcoming year, based on the previous year's ADA, and uses that projection to calculate the amount of money your school will receive. The state sends the money to the school district, which then allocates it to the campus.

In the state's calculation of funding, students are weighted differently, according to their educational needs. More money will be allocated for a student in special education than for a student in regular education, and a student with multiple special education services will have a larger allocation than a student who receives only one special education service, like occupational therapy. Let's say, for instance, that you have 800 students on your campus, and each is automatically allocated $1,000. One student is also designated as needing special education services, so another $500 is allocated to him. Additionally, this same student receives talented and gifted services, so another $100 is allocated to him. Therefore, the total amount that will go to your campus for this particular student is $1,600.

Each year, you will report to your district office how many teachers your campus will need, based on the projected student population. This projection is calculated according to the previous school year's student population, city growth, and other factors. The district's personnel office will assign teachers to your school to teach that population of students and will also assign teacher aides, secretaries, and custodial, cafeteria, and maintenance staff. The amount of money allocated for your school's staff is adjusted up or down according to the numbers of students who are actually on your campus.

Booster and PTA/PTO Funds

Because booster clubs and PTA/PTOs have their own rules and regulations, funds designated for them can sometimes be a headache for administrators. The policies of these organizations are supposed to align with the district's rules and policies, but each booster club or PTA/PTO has an elected board of directors who discuss and vote on items pertaining to a club, program, or organization, like the band, foreign languages, and athletics. A booster club or a PTA/PTO may focus on one area of a campus, like helping the fifth-grade team pay for a field trip, or it may allocate money toward something that the whole campus can use, like new playground equipment. Each organization's board has its own bylaws and/or a constitution that outlines the expectations of the organization and its members. The board also creates and implements organization policies, and it gets to manage its own monies.

Because these organizations are independent entities, you as the school administrator will not have much input or recourse when it comes to the way they spend their money. This usually becomes a problem for an administrator, however, only if misuse or misappropriation of an organization's money is discovered. The school is not really liable, and the only way you can become involved is if you yourself have misused the organization's money in some way. For example, a booster club or PTA/PTO may want to donate or buy a refrigerator for the teachers' lounge as a gift. This purchase is perfectly legal as long as the money is spent on items from vendors approved by the school district's board of trustees, because these vendors have proven that they meet school and district specifications. But if the refrigerator is bought from an unapproved vendor, you could find yourself entangled in a problematic situation.

The best practice in this example would be for the booster club or PTA/PTO to gift the school with the money to buy the refrigerator, and your district will have a form designated for this type of transaction. The booster club or PTA/PTO can donate the money by transferring it to your school's activity fund or by providing cash or a check, and it must also fill out the district's form, showing that the organization is donating money to the school, principal, teacher, or organization for the purchase of a refrigerator. This form and the donation then go to the district-level finance department. Once the money is in your activity fund, you must spend it on the item designated. This process ensures that the actions of both you and the donating organization are legal.

Custodial, Cafeteria, Maintenance, and Transportation Funds

Custodial, cafeteria, maintenance, and transportation staff may be appointed to your campus, but their primary boss will be a district-level director who is well versed in the laws regarding their particular occupation. You may be a secondary or tertiary boss, depending on how many campuses the staff members are assigned to cover. Nevertheless, the funds that are allocated for these personnel may show up in your monthly financial reports, but you most likely will never touch this money, because these types of funds are handled at the district level.

Rental of School Facilities

At times, a church or other community group may wish to rent a building or other facilities on your campus. School rentals are usually handled at the district level, with you providing the requesting group with the proper paperwork. The organization fills out the paperwork and pays the fees attached to the rental, including fees for electricity, water, and custodial services. This transaction of paperwork and money usually occurs at the district level, unless the district prefers to allow school administrators to handle it at the campus level; hence, check your district's policy. You may be asked to provide custodians during the rental event, and usually your only other duties would be to make sure not to schedule any other conflicting event and to send an after-event form to the district office. The rental money collected goes into the district's general fund.

Final Tips

Money can be centrally controlled at the district level or the campus level, depending on your school board's policies. The following tips apply in either case.

- *Your budget must account for everything.* When you receive your annual budget, you will see line items for textbooks, piano repair, band instrument repair, plumbing, maintenance on vending machines, carpet cleaning, and so on. Every item purchased and every service that occurs on your campus are paid for through your budget. When a teacher needs a computer technician to fix her computer, you have money in your budget that pays for that. When a light fixture has to be replaced, you have money to pay for the fixture and the electrician's time. Remind everyone on your campus that nothing is free. Everything has a price and is paid for through the school's budget.

- *Trust your secretary.* A principal's secretary can be the best resource to keep track of the budget for you, so trust one who really understands all the various codes that appear in the budget and how they work. If you are lucky enough to choose your own secretary, choose one who knows the budget codes and relevant laws very well. Even if you don't get to choose your secretary, work with him or her to learn about the district's rules for collecting and spending money.

- *Understand quarterly reports.* Anything that you must sign must be reviewed! Quarterly local, state, and federal documents that must be submitted to the district finance office are usually prepared by the principal's secretary or designee and must be signed by an administrator for authenticity. Your signature denotes that you know how money has been spent and on what items. Review these quarterly documents carefully so that you understand what you are signing. These documents show the spending patterns of your campus, including each fund's expenditures and current balance. After you send these documents to the district finance office, district staff will review them and compare them with the district's documentation for your campus, then send you a report showing what information is aligned and what is not. If there is any discrepancy, you will have to work with your secretary to bring your documents into alignment with the district's.

- *Keep everything, and document everything.* Your district office will always keep documentation of the funds allotted to your campus, so you and your secretary must maintain thorough documentation in your office as well. Once, a new principal arrived on campus and threw away everything in the front office—even the ledgers, because she did not know what they were. (This was at a time when records were still kept by hand in ledger books.) Later, during a professional development class on finance and budgets, she and her secretary, who was also new to the campus, found out that the ledgers should have been kept for planning the next year's budget. Without the ledgers, they had to

scramble to figure out the campus's money situation in order to prepare the school's budget. The lessons learned: Don't throw anything
away from the previous administration, and document everything concerning money allocated to your campus. These days financial records
are maintained on computers, but you still must keep your computer
files and handwritten documentation current and well protected.

- **Purchase orders.** Purchase orders are the means for gaining access to
  the money allocated to your campus, so that you can make appropriate
  purchases. As documentation, purchase orders form a crucial paper
  trail showing how your school's money has been spent. The district
  office must approve purchase orders. After it has approved an order
  and confirmed that your school has the money to spend, it will fill
  the order either from the school district's warehouse or through an
  approved vendor. In some cases, the approved purchase order will be
  returned to the campus, and the secretary will order what is needed.
  The secretary signs for the item when it is delivered, and keeps the
  documentation of this final leg of the purchase order's journey.

■ ■ ■

A school's financial and budgetary matters are very intricate and most of
the time are centrally managed at the district level. All you really have to do
is keep track of how much money you started the year with, what you spent
throughout the year, and how much money you have left at the end of the
year. And you must be vigilant in adhering to policies and laws related to the
administration of your school's financial matters. You and your secretary must
keep tabs on all of this and then periodically check your ledgers to make sure
they balance.

CHAPTER 6

Welcoming Parents and the Community into Your School

Parental and community involvement will affect your campus directly and indirectly and will definitely play a big role in your evaluation as an administrator. Document how you involve parents in the school lives of their children and how you encourage community members to become a part of your school campus. This involvement may be a challenging task, and you will need to be a model for your teachers in partnering with parents and community members.

Involving Parents

When you are creating partnerships with parents, one major idea to keep in mind is that time is precious to parents. Some parents have demanding jobs and are not able to come to the campus during school hours. Others may have multiple jobs that do not leave them any time to visit their children's school. If you have students on your campus who are bused to school, that may be a sign that some of their parents don't have transportation to the school. Understanding the dilemmas that parents face will help you know what to expect.

To promote parents' involvement with schools, some businesses allow their employees to leave work without penalty in order to attend conferences with their children's teachers or other school personnel. In school districts that include military families, post commanders and brigade officers sometimes release parents on days that parent-teacher meetings or other events are happening at their children's school. Additionally, some post commanders release all personnel in the early afternoon on certain days to allow for family time. In some cities, businesses do the same, giving parents time to address their children's needs.

Thus, it is necessary to ensure that any time a parent spends on your campus is meaningful. If a parent volunteers on campus, then you and your staff must arrange gratifying experiences for them, such as mentoring and tutoring students. Bear in mind, however, that some parents may view making photo-copies, cutting out bulletin board art, or categorizing a class library as a waste of their time, while others may feel more comfortable not working with students directly and may ask to do such tasks.

Remind all of your staff who work with parent volunteers that student grades and course work, as well as any documents that contain student information, must not be a part of tasks that a volunteer fulfills. Ensure that federal statutes—such as the Family Educational Rights and Privacy Act of 1974 (FERPA), which addresses confidentiality issues—are followed. Review with your staff the pitfalls of sharing confidential information and the potential ramifications of doing so, such as the sanctioning of teacher certification. Additionally, students in special programs are protected by federal mandates (e.g., IDEA for special education or Title 1 for schools that qualify), which means that educators who violate them may be prosecuted at the federal level.

FERPA, also known as the Buckley Amendment, focuses on the privacy of certain information pertaining to students and their families. Briefly, FERPA gives rights to students and parents to inspect and review records, amend any record, give or not give consent for disclosure of information found in the records, and submit a grievance or complaint to any educational agency, including the US Department of Education. If a family believes that a violation has occurred and decides to sue, the case will be heard at the federal court level. This law is easy to obey: private information about students and their families may be shared only if there is an educational need to do so, and in some cases the permission of the student and/or parents is required.

Involving the Community

You will have many opportunities to participate in various community organizations, such as the Lions Club or the Rotary Club. Such organizations perform community service and are excellent points of contact for you to have when your school needs help from the community. Businesses and local colleges and universities also may wish to donate money, merchandise, mentoring, facilities, and other resources to your school. Some of your students' parents will be associated with these organizations or businesses and may be able to initiate contact between them and your school. Additionally, these parents may serve as liaisons between organizations or businesses and provide certain resources, like guest speakers. For instance, a child's father who is a city police officer might arrange for McGruff the Crime Dog to visit the campus.

Donations of money should be placed in one of your school's activity funds. Monetary donations can usually be spent on almost anything, but be sure to follow your district's guidelines. Merchandise such as classroom supplies, paper products, and food may be donated for a special occasion, like an open house or a school dinner. Some schools have partnered with food chains to promote a family dinner night either at the school or at the food chain's premises. The money earned through the purchase of food at this type of event is shared with the school, sometimes as much as 15 percent of the proceeds. Whatever kinds of donations you receive, you must report them to the school district's finance department.

Another way that local businesses, colleges, and universities can become involved in your campus is through mentoring and tutoring. Some special programs—like AVID (Advancement Via Individual Determination), for example—encourage high school students to pursue a college education. Partnerships with local businesses may entice employees to visit your campus to mentor students and to make presentations on topics in their fields. Mentoring students, whether individually or in a group, benefits them by giving them one-on-one time with a person who is attentive and supportive. Expert presenters can show students the importance of an occupation. Sometimes a single presentation is life-changing for students, inspiring them to succeed in their school endeavors and beyond. In addition, service organizations, hospitals, restaurants, and mechanics, for example, may have much to offer young students. Especially at the high school level, these organizations can partner with the career and technology education (CATE) department to provide on-the-job and real-life opportunities for students. In addition, several food chains partner with special education classrooms to bring students on-site for job experience, like busing tables or preparing pizza boxes for takeout.

As you look for ways to involve your community and provide your students with varied experiences, do not forget the community's retired persons. They may have much to share and contribute. One retired army general visits a high school daily, helping in any way he can. He has served as a mentor, a tutor, and a lunch monitor. Another retiree reads to an elementary class every Thursday morning and spends time with the students as a grandfather figure, telling them stories about the "old days."

Steps for Increasing Parental and Community Involvement

Parents and community members will expect great things from you as a campus leader, and they will assume that you are very knowledgeable about your school, its needs, and the family and community members who help support it. Taking these simple steps will help increase involvement in your school.

- ***Step 1: Understand the community.*** One of the first things you should do after you are promoted to an administrative position is to drive around the community. Look for the different types of businesses, homes, and activities that surround your campus. Find out if the city bus, subway, or other forms of transportation stop nearby. Notice if the housing in the area includes homes, apartments, and/or hotels and if students have easy or difficult access to the campus. Be cognizant of those students who are dropped off at school well before you or anyone else reports for duty. Know which students walk, drive, take a bus, or take a day-care van to school and which students go to a day care center or to another home before they see their parents after school. Also learn which students work at businesses in your community.

    Visit the many places your students and teachers frequent, like churches and community centers. Discover which state agencies can provide services to your campus, like Job Corps or Family and Adult Services, both of which can help students and parents. Find out what businesses are willing to donate to your school, visiting them and talking with their managers. Tell them about the great things that are happening on your campus, and create partnerships with them. Get to know community leaders, and ask them how they might help your campus stay successful.

- ***Step 2: Offer multiple invitations.*** Simply invite parents to the school when you see them in person, and also communicate with them through email, texts, letters, the school website, the school marquee, and phone calls. Get them interested by bragging about what is happening at your campus, being specific in what the students and teachers are doing. Welcome parents onto the campus, and let them know about upcoming special events, such as an open house, booster club meetings, student presentations and competitions, concerts, plays, and so on. Invite them to volunteer, and tell them about the many ways they can help on campus. Let them know they can participate by becoming a member of the Parent Teacher Association/Organization (PTA/PTO); volunteering to monitor the lunchroom, recess, or a homeroom; chaperoning a field trip, a school dance, or a science fair; or joining a booster club.

    Some schools specifically invite a certain population to share in the successes of the students and teachers. Events like Muffins for Mom, Doughnuts for Dad, or Gummi Bears for Grandparents are special opportunities for the students and teachers to honor one person from each family.

For community members, invitations to school festivals, spring flings, and family potluck dinner nights will help create awareness of your school's exciting projects and accomplishments and will lead to partnerships and a sense of unity. Such events might give community members an opportunity to advertise as well, but make sure you follow your district's guidelines when allowing them to advertise or to sell any items on your campus.

- ***Step 3: Entice with incentives.*** There are many fun ways to inspire parents and community members to make a donation of some kind. One way is through incentives, which should be specific and meaningful. At a middle school, for example, parents were asked to attend at least three school events throughout the year, such as an open house, a parent-teacher conference, and a science fair. At the end of the year, the parents who had participated were given a school spirit T-shirt that bore the name of the school and the words "I support my child's school."

    To involve the community, a high school business teacher created a partnership with the local nursing home. In order to earn 150 hours of community service at the nursing home, which was a part of the course expectations, students read to the residents and performed plays and organized dances for them. The students enjoyed the assignment and did such a great job that the local newspaper and news stations highlighted how happy the nursing home residents were, and a local doctor commented that the happiness of the residents had improved their health.

- ***Step 4: Thank parents and community members.*** Whether the contributions that parents or community members make to your school are large or small, remember to thank them specifically and genuinely for what they did for the school. If they donated money, thank them for it, mentioning the amount they gave and how your campus plans to spend it. If a parent mentored a student throughout the year, and the student improved academically because of it, then state that in your thank-you note. If possible, include a school pride item—like a mug, a pen, a T-shirt, or a key chain with the school logo—along with the thank-you note, to emphasize your campus's appreciation.

    A thank-you can also come in the form of a breakfast, a luncheon, a dinner, or an awards night where you publicly thank volunteers for their service, stating exactly what they did for the students, teachers, and campus as a whole. Ask the local newspaper to report how grateful you are for all of the individuals, businesses, and educational institutions that support your school, and provide a list of those who have donated to the school. Other possibilities are to have each class create a thank-you poster, film a video and post it on the school's website, or make a banner expressing appreciation to the donors and hang it outside the school where the public can see it.

- ***Step 5: Stay in contact.*** Maintain contact with the parents and community members who have become involved with your campus, and ask them if they would like to continue to volunteer in the future. Make yourself a contact list that includes all of these individuals and businesses, cataloguing what they donated and when, what their donation was used for, and their skills or resources, and refer to this list as needed throughout the year and in coming years.

Following this action plan will increase parental and community involvement, especially as you modify and fine-tune each step to fit the needs of your school.

Campus Access and Professional Development

Before allowing any volunteer to gain access to your campus, be sure to check into your school board's policies regarding volunteers. To keep your school safe and secure, allow only persons who are adequately vetted to be volunteers or mentors. This means that all potential volunteers and mentors must undergo a background check and fingerprinting to ensure that there is no record of criminal activity in their past, including sex offenses, that would preclude them from being allowed on a school campus.

Once parents and community members have been vetted, it is a good idea to give them training on what is expected of them while they are on campus. For example, spending an hour with volunteers to relay what lunch duty consists of is a good idea. Explaining the cafeteria rules, the procedures for reporting a Student Code of Conduct violation, and how to identify students by name and grade level is necessary so that volunteers feel they are a part of the campus and so that they will be fair to all of the students on the campus. Finally, inform the volunteers of the dates and times they are to be on the campus and how they should check in and out when entering and leaving the campus.

Providing volunteers with a job description or a contract of some kind that states what types of professional behavior and dress are expected of them may be helpful in the long run, and you should have them sign it. The more detailed and explicit the information you give volunteers, the better the chances that everyone will have positive experiences. Having a detailed written description can also facilitate the process for dismissing a volunteer for violation of the job description or contract.

All campus staff should encourage parental and community involvement, and to do so, they will need to be informed about the vetting process and training that volunteers must go through. Additionally, school personnel should understand how to interact with people who enter the campus and want to be a part of the campus family. Hence, professional development that focuses on customer care will help all campus personnel interact appropriately with both parents and community members. Customer care training covers how to meet and greet, communicate professionally, and work toward positive interactions with clarity and purpose.

■ ■ ■

Gaining and maintaining parental and community involvement can be a fun aspect of your job as an administrator, because you will have the opportunity to meet many people who will want to help your campus be successful. Think of this as your chance to practice public relations. You will establish rewarding relationships with the public and create partnerships that can be very beneficial to the entire school family.

Leading with Vigilance

■ ■ ■

CHAPTER 7

Keeping the School Safe

The scariest—there is not another word that truly describes this—part of your job as an administrator will be your responsibility for keeping your campus safe and orderly. The scariness comes when you realize that you cannot absolutely guarantee anyone's safety on a campus, because you cannot guarantee that every human being who sets foot on your campus will behave in a civil and harmless manner. To help prevent unsafe and uncivil conduct on your campus, this chapter outlines what school safety may look like and how to prepare your campus for the unexpected.

Maintaining a Secure Campus

Simply stated, a safe campus is one on which every possible measure has been taken to secure facilities from harm. School safety also depends on the people who are on a campus, and their determination to safeguard it. Follow the steps below to make your campus as secure as possible.

- One of the first things you must do as a new administrator is to explore the entire campus, going inside each building and outbuilding, familiarizing yourself with each building's layout and contents, and walking around the perimeter and grounds of the campus. By doing this, you will learn what kinds of hiding places there may be, like alcoves or stairwells, and locate any areas that may be unsecure. Know each and every corner of your campus, so that you will be aware when something seems unusual or out of place and so that you can identify and correct unsafe conditions in areas that could be potential sites for dangerous or illegal activities.

- All staff, but especially administrators, must ritualistically observe and check each part of a campus and keep a log of the items and conditions that should be present and any discrepancies or changes in them. Each morning, walk around your campus, no matter how large, to ensure that all is secure. The great bonus of doing this is that it will increase your visibility to teachers, students, and parents, who will see you and interact with you.

- Enlist teachers and other personnel on the campus to be observant of each area that they frequent. This will help them notice if anything is out of sorts or needs repair.

- Keep all nonessential doors locked. This may be easier said than done, but try to keep only the front doors to the front office open. On some campuses, there are several buildings in use during the day, and students and teachers may come in and out of various doors. If at all possible, maintain security at these entry points by keeping them locked and giving teachers door keys or ID or keypad pass codes. On some campuses, especially high schools, students don't always adhere to policies about keeping doors closed (and automatically locked) after they enter a building, and they may even prop a door open for a friend. Be diligent in noticing this type of behavior, and address it accordingly.

- The buddy system always works well for both students and teachers. If students and teachers must walk from one building to the next or to a parking lot, having them walk with a buddy is a worthwhile safety precaution.

- Video cameras are essential to keeping a campus secure. Not only will they help you become aware of unsafe conditions or activities, but they will also shed light on violations to the Student Code of Conduct (SCOC) or the employee handbook. Having video records of violations can also be useful.

- Phones and/or walkie-talkies are a must in every room. All administrators and all employees on a campus should have each other's cell phone and office/room numbers, recorded on a central list that is public to all on a campus. Additionally, all staff should keep their phones with them at all times, in case of an emergency. If possible, have a walkie-talkie system for administrators and their staff, so that you can communicate with one another at any time. Having code words for particular kinds of situations may help convey urgency. For example, an assistant principal at an elementary school and the secretary had code words for the most common occurrences on their campus: "Your Sonic Blast is here!" meant that an angry parent was in the office; and "Bevo is in trouble" meant that a fight was occurring in the lunchroom.

- Emergency emails, texts, and alerts should be sent out at least monthly by the district and the campus as practice drills. At the campus level, ask your teachers to sign up to receive these communications on their school and home computers, cell phones, tablets, and any other electronic device they may use. Enlist your technology personnel to help you with this task.

All of this advice is great if you have the funds to buy what is needed to carry it out. Security equipment and services can be expensive, but teaching your teachers and all other personnel on a campus how to be diligently aware and observant on your campus at all times is security that needs no purchase.

No Guarantees

Unfortunately, as an administrator, you cannot guarantee that everyone on a campus will always be safe and free from harm. You cannot guarantee that weapons will not make their way onto your campus, because some students and employees may arm themselves with weapons if they feel threatened. For example, there have been many instances when students who have been bullied have brought a gun or a prohibited knife with a large blade with them to school in order to handle the bully. In turn, many teachers legally carry guns or knives in order to feel safe.

What you *can* guarantee is that you will do your very best to keep each and every person on your campus safe and secure. There are many ways to keep this promise, including the following.

1. Create a campus discipline committee of five to nine members. Charge this committee with determining ways to keep the campus safe. The committee's tasks should include creating SCOC lesson plans to be taught throughout the year, creating crisis plans, recommending security purchases (e.g., video cameras and walkie-talkies), and keeping track of discipline issues. Committee members should consistently communicate with staff, students, parents, and central office personnel regarding strategies implemented to establish a safe and orderly campus.

2. Communicate! Let everyone know what you and your staff are doing to keep the campus free from harm. Communicate as much as possible about campus safety with your teachers and other employees, students, parents, the central office, and community members. Talk, visit, email, and call individuals, and post information and announcements on the school's marquee and/or website. The campus discipline

committee can help you with this communication. By sending out reminders through various communications, you will keep everyone informed about security measures and what you expect from teachers, students, and visitors on campus.

3. Metal detectors are excellent devices to deter students from bringing guns and other weapons to school. However, these devices are very expensive to use, maintain, and store. If you are able to contract the use of them, communicate to everyone on campus how they will be used, how often, and why.

4. "Search and seize" only when you have reliable information about a possible violation of either the SCOC or the penal code. In some states, in order to search a student and his or her property, you must have at least a suspicion that is based on information that has come to your attention. For example, a student or teacher may tell you that he or she heard about someone holding drugs, or you may receive a tip from the school's crime prevention hotline. In other states, reasonable doubt must be ascertained. Although this reasonable doubt does not have to parallel what is expected from police officers, more than just hearsay is needed to prompt a search and seizure. (More on this topic is provided later in this chapter, under "The Discipline Process" in the section "Student Code of Conduct.")

5. Review the SCOC frequently yourself and with your staff, students, and parents. First, teach the teachers exactly what you need them to know about the SCOC and why enforcing the code is important in maintaining a safe and orderly campus. Next, have your discipline committee create relevant lesson plans, each focusing on a rule from the code and the consequences for breaking that rule. Then, schedule the lessons to be taught during the first week of school, after school holidays, and throughout the year, as reminders of expected behavior. Giving the teachers lesson plans and a schedule for delivering them serves two purposes: everyone will be teaching the same lesson on the same day, and teachers will have fewer lesson plans to write themselves during the first week of school.

6. Encourage teachers and other personnel to be hall coordinators for each period or time of the day, to ensure that all students and teachers are safe and accounted for. Monitoring the bathrooms too is a good idea, since cameras can't be present, and fights, drug sales, and the like are sometimes associated with bathroom breaks.

7. Whether to have a closed campus or an open one is an issue that many school boards face annually when addressing the needs of high schools. Especially during lunchtime, high schools become very busy

and chaotic because of the many students leaving and returning to campus. On a closed campus, all students are fed on campus and do not have permission to leave for lunch. On an open campus, students may come and go at will during their lunchtime. This arrangement may generate administrative challenges for maintaining a secure campus. Educators or other personnel should be posted at all doors where students enter and exit and in the student parking lot to help keep an open campus safe.

8. Have school resource officers and/or city police officers as a constant presence on campus. At many high schools, these officers are usually present. But at elementary and middle schools, they may not be present unless they are specifically called to the campus. Armed personnel enhance campus security, but like you, they can't be everywhere at once. If they are making their rounds and a crime occurs elsewhere on campus, they should not be blamed. Instead, review how the crime occurred, and take steps to prevent similar crimes in the future.

9. IDs should be worn by every person on the campus. Color-code the IDs to identify students by grade level, put their picture and name on both sides of the ID, and make horizontal IDs for staff and vertical IDs for students. This is a quick visual way to recognize who is supposed to be on your campus and who may be trespassing. Additionally, IDs can be used for buying lunches, purchasing school spirit items, paying for course fees, and obtaining many other things from a school campus.

10. Know who's on your campus at all times, as much as possible. If substitutes, parent volunteers, community mentors, tutors, or any other visitors are on your campus, be aware of them and know their reason for being there. After they check in with you and/or the designated personnel, give them IDs that identify them and their role.

11. Have a system in place for visitors to sign in and out. Many school districts have implemented a visitor management system, such as Raptor, from a commercial vendor. Such systems track who enters and exits a campus through an electronic system that requires each visitor to present a driver's license or other state-issued ID. Before persons are allowed to enter the main building of a campus, they may need to ring a doorbell, identify themselves, and state their business on campus. Then they must properly check in with the front office staff. They must also check out at the front office and let the office staff know that they are leaving the campus.

12. Be sure to identify sex offenders who reside near the school either by working with your SRO to find the information or by accessing your city's or county's website and searching for "sex offenders." At times, you may find that a parent is a sex offender. In such a case, follow your school board's policy on how to handle the situation. For example, some schools will not allow parents who are sex offenders to come to campus unannounced, and once on campus, they are escorted until they depart.

13. After you have established a system for identifying both personnel and visitors on your campus, make sure everyone follows it. If district personnel wear a district badge on campus, some campus systems accept the badge as a valid form of ID, but no matter who these individuals are or where they are from, they must still properly check in as everyone else does. Sometimes district personnel may feel that they don't need to sign in because they are wearing a badge, but don't be afraid to question them and have them sign in. If necessary, issue a school ID to them, so that your staff knows they have been cleared through the main office. Additionally, have your teachers ask anyone on campus without a proper ID if he or she has checked in at the front office. If not, then the teacher should have the person escorted to the office. Support your teachers in this effort.

School Resource Officers

One of the best components of a comprehensive security system is the school resource officer (SRO). An SRO can be found in most high schools, and often more than one is present. SROs can also be assigned to middle and elementary schools, dividing their time between them. They are peace officers, which means they have attended a police academy, have been trained to use a weapon (gun and Taser), and have been granted the authority to issue citations and make arrests by becoming certified in their state.

An SRO provides school-based policing education and is involved in maintaining campus security. SROs are also concerned with crime prevention, teaching how to abide by the law and what the law actually means. Like educators, SROs are not untouchable or infallible.

Get to know the SROs assigned to your campus and treat them as part of your staff. Invite them to staff meetings, luncheons, and the like, and help them feel welcomed. SROs can give you up-to-date information on students and teachers, especially those who have been arrested over the weekend. They will be able to tell you which students are on probation or have warrants. To implement a successful SRO program, an administrator needs to consider five major points.

1. Having an SRO on campus allows for the visibility of a police officer in a setting other than in a police vehicle or on TV making arrests. Police officers are commonly seen patrolling in their vehicles, and sometimes a city police officer will be present at a movie theater or a city council meeting. With an SRO program, a visible law enforcement presence can now be extended to the school campus, football games, school board meetings, and any other place where it is needed within a school environment.

2. SROs provide law enforcement advice to staff and students. SROs should have a friendly and approachable demeanor on a campus, so that students and staff perceive them as persons who can help, whether to assist during an emergency or to counsel those on a campus who have questions about legal and personal matters.

3. SROs serve as a security and law enforcement presence in situations involving illegal or dangerous activities. When you have to perform a search and seizure of a student's property, the SRO can be ready to take an enforcement action, as needed. When a fight breaks out in the lunchroom and hundreds of students rush to see what's happening, an SRO can help the administrative staff keep order and maintain safety.

4. You must choose the right person to be an SRO for your campus. When a police officer is considered for a position within a police department, an extensive background check and psychological testing are completed, and fingerprints are taken and entered in a database. If the school district does not have its own police department and needs to contract with another, such as the city police department, the district administration must work closely with the law enforcement agency that employs the SRO, and should insist on obtaining a secondary background check, set of fingerprints, and psychological testing to confirm the records the police department has on the SRO. Ensure that your school's psychologist understands that you are looking, not for an SRO who can simply pass the police psychological test, but someone who also has an honest personal life so that educators won't have to worry about an inappropriate relationship developing on campus.

5. The SRO should be given a separate office, away from any administrative offices, with enough space for performing his or her duties, which may include fingerprinting a suspected criminal, weighing and authenticating drugs, and reviewing camera data. This private office can also help students and staff feel comfortable when they are providing crime prevention tips.

Many school districts have their own police department, but others contract SRO services from the city or county's law enforcement agency. Usually, at the district level, the assistant superintendent in charge of hiring the SROs will have firsthand contact with the law enforcement agency and will give you information on the person who will be assigned to your campus.

The issues that an SRO will face largely depend on the type of campus they are assigned. At an elementary campus, the SRO may be asked to read to students, to visit the classrooms and give presentations on safety, and to walk around the campus to ensure everyone's safety. At middle schools, SROs help the faculty keep the campus secure and may be more of a counselor to the students, including reminding them that at their age they can be subject to arrests and jail time for lawbreaking. An SRO at the high school level must pay attention to how students behave, what they are saying, which students have vehicles, what students are doing between classes, which students are on probation, whether the campus and its facilities are secure, and so on. They also may provide law enforcement instruction to the staff, such as alerting them to which fad drugs that kids are using or why they are wearing a certain type of clothing. At both the middle and high school levels, the SRO may provide assemblies or class presentations on current issues like bullying, drug use, alcohol use, driving safety, and criminal law.

Types of Law Enforcement Personnel

In some school districts, a variety of law enforcement personnel may serve as SROs, such as city or county police officers or security guards, and each of these law enforcers has distinctive characteristics. A school district SRO is a peace officer, may enforce the SCOC and the penal code, carries a gun, a Taser, and/or a baton, and may make arrests. City and county police officers will enforce the penal code but will merely inform the administration about SCOC violations. They, too, are peace officers who carry a gun, Taser, and/or baton, and may make arrests. Security guards are not peace officers but have been trained to observe an assigned area and enforce an organization's rules. Security guards will uphold any rule or law that is assigned to them, but they do not have any legislative authority to make arrests, except those that regular citizens can make (for felonies and breaches of the peace). They may be armed only if they are certified by their state to be armed, and in the event a citizen's arrest is made, they would need to call for police officers.

City police officers who are not assigned to your campus can still be of assistance. Some city officers perform community policing. They are assigned to areas within the city, and they patrol the neighborhoods, which can include the schools. If you don't have an SRO regularly assigned to your campus, then contact the police department to find out who patrols your school's neighborhood and community. Then invite the officers to your campus and introduce them to your staff, students, and parents. Let them know of any concerns you or your staff may have, ask how you can help make the campus more secure, and accept their advice for ensuring the safety of your staff and students. Remember to always follow the school district's chain of command before calling the city police, and gain permission to call as needed.

Working with Law Enforcement Personnel

The chief of police and the school superintendent should have a working relationship. The statutes in many states require the police department and the school district to work together to keep the schools and the surrounding communities safe. For example, when the police department publishes its weekly blotter of arrests and criminal activity, a police designee will notify the school district's central office if students and/or employees show up on the blotter. Additionally, if a student or employee is arrested, the police designee will inform the district designee about the details of the arrest. The district can use this information to pursue appropriate disciplinary actions.

One bit of advice when working with police officers is to befriend them and work with them to keep the peace. They are the law enforcement experts. At one high school, a principal told both the SROs and the city police officers assigned to her campus that she was the boss and if any arrest, search, seizure, warrant service, or other police activity needed to occur on campus, they would need to get her approval first. One police officer promptly told her that the city and state were his employers, that any penal code violation was subject to immediate police intervention, and that the principal's permission would not be sought. This set up a power struggle, and throughout that school year the principal continued to assert her position as the campus boss, and the police officers continued to ignore her. The lesson here is to work with those who are trying to help you keep your campus safe, and to develop good communication with them.

Along with the police department chief, the city's fire department chief will also make contact with the superintendent and school campuses regarding fire hazards and how to keep your campus compliant with fire-related regulations. Heed all advice from the fire chief, and be sure that you are always following the city and state codes.

When the police or fire fighters are called to your campus, especially through a 911 call, they will take control of the situation. Be prepared to give up your authority to them, no matter how difficult that may feel, because control of your campus officially stops being yours once the police and other emergency responders become involved.

In dire situations, the school district is tasked with collaborating with police, fire, and medical personnel. In the case of an extreme criminal event or other emergency, such as a shooting or an explosion on campus, the district must have a plan of action ready to implement. This plan usually goes to the chief law enforcement officer in the district's jurisdiction for review and approval and is then distributed to police, fire, and medical personnel. Having a plan in place for dealing with a dire event increases the likelihood that those affected will be helped quickly. Check your state codes for the required elements of this plan of action, and explore the websites at the end of this chapter for help with preparing a plan.

During dire situations, certain areas must be designated for particular uses in response to the emergency, such as a command post, a triage area, and a point of contact for school personnel, students, and parents. From the command post, the incident commander will direct the emergency response and see to the dissemination of information. Depending on the situation, the commander might be the superintendent or the principal, but if an active shooter is present on a campus, a designated police officer will be the incident commander. If a harmful chemical or biological substance is released on a campus, a hazmat (hazardous materials) responder or a medical doctor might be the incident commander. Only essential personnel (e.g., SWAT police officers, medical personnel, principal, superintendent) will be allowed in or near the command post area.

A triage area is usually located away from the danger, because it is a makeshift first aid station for determining those in most need of medical attention. Only police, medical, fire, and possibly school personnel will have access to this area. The point of contact for school personnel, students, and parents may be in a nearby school gym or community center. School administrators need to take control of this area and should communicate with all of those needing information. More on an Incident Command System can be viewed at the Federal Emergency Management Agency (FEMA) website, at www.fema.gov/incident-command-system/. Although this site is geared toward national emergencies, the concepts can be applied to campus emergencies.

The Student Code of Conduct

The Student Code of Conduct (SCOC) is the approved "law of the land" from your district's school board. The SCOC is aligned with state statutes that outline the topics it must cover, like suspensions and expulsions. The code also will cover the kinds of infractions that may occur on a campus. These infractions are usually listed in a hierarchy, from most severe to minor. The following are examples of infractions or violations that may be included in an SCOC.

1. Expellable violations are those that are both SCOC offenses and felony offenses, such as kidnapping, murder, or indecency with a child. In many states, the commission of an expellable offense does not mean that you send a student to the streets. Students must have access to an education even when they are expelled; hence, they are sent to a school-approved alternative placement for discipline, where they will receive both behavioral and academic instruction. Consequences for this level of violations may include a phone call home, in-school suspension (ISS), out-of-school suspension (OSS), a police citation, a police arrest, a discipline hearing, and/or time in jail. Expellable offenses trigger mandatory alternative placements. This means that a discipline hearing (discussed below) will be convened and a recommendation for placement in a disciplinary alternative education program (DAEP) will occur. If the penal code has been violated, a student may be arrested and placed in jail or a JJAEP (juvenile justice alternative education program).

2. Serious violations parallel crimes that are listed in most state penal codes. These types of violations may include sexual assault, physical assault of a school employee or another student, or sexting. Consequences may consist of a phone call home, ISS, OSS, a police citation, a police arrest, a discipline hearing for determining placement in a DAEP, placement in a JJAEP, and/or time in jail. Serious violations usually trigger mandatory alternative placements, which means a discipline hearing will take place.

3. Major infractions are significant and usually are committed by only a few students. Major infractions may include fighting, use of profanity, insubordination, persistent misconduct, and harassment of others. Consequences may be a phone call home, detention, demerits, ISS, OSS, a police citation, or a police arrest. Some major violations may lead to a school hearing and a recommendation from the administration for student placement in a DAEP. These type of violations may be referred to as discretionary, which means that the administration can decide whether or not the student will be referred to an alternative placement or if campus discipline interventions (e.g., a behavior intervention plan, or BIP) would be put in place.

4. Minor violations are those that are possibly seen every day, and at one time or another most students will receive a warning or a minor consequence associated with this type of violation. Minor violations may encompass failure to adhere to the dress code, tardies, ID badge violations, and truancies. Consequences could include a warning, a phone

call home, a time-out, detention, demerits, or ISS. Consistent minor violations, or persistent misconduct, would become major violations for which a hearing may be held.

The various levels of violations may parallel each other, and you may find the same offenses listed in each area. This is purposefully done by many school boards, to allow the administration the professional judgment to choose the appropriate consequence for a student, based on seriousness of the infraction, the student's age and demeanor during interrogation, frequency of misconduct, and effect of the violation on the learning environment. Hence, a kindergartener may punch another student out of frustration, while a senior in high school may punch another student in order to start a fight. Both have violated the SCOC, and an assault of another student is usually listed as both a serious offense and a major offense, with consequences that could involve a police citation and arrest. However, the context for the punch, the student's age, and all other relevant information may lead you to discipline the kindergartner in a much different manner from how you would discipline the senior.

Let's start from the beginning to understand how you will go about dealing with discipline on your campus. Discipline starts with making rules and informing everyone on campus of those rules. First, you must teach your teachers how to read the SCOC and how to use it. They should never be afraid to discipline students, because the school board has approved that all educators may discipline students according to the SCOC. Second, you must teach the students how to read and understand the types of violations and consequences listed in the SCOC.

As stated earlier, your campus discipline committee should create lesson plans to be taught specifically during the first week of school and then throughout the year. These lessons should be detailed and clear, giving students examples of what an infraction looks like and examples of what it doesn't look like. The various consequences for an infraction should be explained, especially consequences that involve the police.

These lesson plans could also be offered as a news story by a journalism class during the school's morning television news—for instance, during Channel One time. Additionally, they could be published as a news item in the school newspaper. Some schools have also presented the lesson plans in assemblies, with the teachers and administrators acting out examples of acceptable and unacceptable behavior. Other schools have produced a video with students portraying an SCOC violation, the referral process for the student, and the district hearing process. This video was then made available on the school's website and shown during the school's morning television news.

Make an impact on the students about the seriousness of the SCOC and the importance of following it. One good argument to make to students in support of your enforcement of the SCOC is that the SCOC parallels society's code of conduct, the penal code. Students must understand that having a safe, secure, and orderly campus also helps keep them safe, secure, and orderly in society.

The Discipline Process

The discipline process can be fast and easy, or it can be a laborious, time-consuming journey involving many people. The process starts with a violation of the SCOC and continues with a discipline referral, administrative intervention, and a consequence. There can be many steps to disciplining a student, and each step is explained in this section. Assistant principals are usually assigned the disciplinary duties on a campus; therefore, the administrator mentioned in this section will refer to the assistant principal or the person who serves as the campus disciplinarian.

The most important idea to remember when working with the SCOC is due process—consistently carrying out the discipline process according to the established SCOC. Due process gives every person in a situation a chance to tell his or her side of the story, while also being treated fairly. In this way, you will find out what happened during an event, who was involved, how it affected the learning environment, and what violations of the SCOC and/or the penal code took place. After all of this information has been gathered about an event, then you can make a professional decision about which consequence is appropriate to apply.

Due process occurs constantly throughout the day and school year. For example, a student is not wearing her school-issued ID around her neck, as is the expectation. This is a minor offense, yet it is a violation of the SCOC. You ask the student where her ID is and tell her to put it on, which she does. What you did was to perform due process, by giving the student a chance to produce her ID and put it on. You gave the student a chance to comply, and you gave her the benefit of the doubt that failing to wear her ID was not done on purpose.

Let's look at a lengthier example of a discipline issue to get another view of due process in action. Seventh grader Burris has brought a butcher knife to school in order to protect himself from a bully on campus. You receive a tip from Burris's friend, who tells you that Burris has a knife in his locker and plans to use it during lunchtime in the courtyard to attack his bully. What are your first steps?

- Have Burris's friend write a statement that details the tip (how he knows about the knife, where the knife is currently, and the intended purpose of the knife), and then have Burris sign and date the statement.

- While Burris's friend is writing his statement, contact your SRO or another administrator and have that person go with you to find Burris.

Never follow up on a tip about a weapon or drugs by calling the student out of class to come to your office, because on the way to your office, the student may get rid of any evidence. Instead, go to the student, ask him or her to come with you *and* to bring all belongings, and walk with the student back to your office. Have the student walk *in front* of you on the way to your office. Students who do have prohibited items in their possession will try to rid themselves of it, so keeping them in front of you helps you see if this is tried.

• In your office or in a secure area, perform a search of Burris and his property. Let Burris know that you received a tip about him having a weapon on campus, but there is no need to tell him who gave the tip. Follow your school board policies, and understand the two ways that a search can be done. The first way is for you to pat a student down and go through the student's backpack, purse, or other belongings. You do the actual looking and searching, touching everything that the student has in his or her possession. This helps you have first access to a weapon or any other prohibited item, before the student has a chance to get it and possibly cause harm or dispose of it. The second way is to allow the student to do the pat-down and the search of belongings himself or herself. When using this option, you must stand right next to the student as the pat-down and search are done, and when you see a prohibited item, then you can ask the student to remove his or her hands and/or step away from the item. Remember to search everything thoroughly, because students can be very inventive when hiding prohibited items. Also, check with your SRO about the best hiding places that students use, especially the less obvious ones. The following are some examples:

  • *Mouth*—Students have been known to hide razor blades in their mouth, so have the student open his or her mouth during a search.

  • *Hair*—Students with thick or "big" hair can hide drugs or razors in it.

  • *Caps or hats*—If you allow caps to be worn during school hours, under the cap or inside it is an opportune area to store prohibited items.

  • *Ears*—Small vials can be glued or taped behind the ears.

  • *Pens/pencils/markers*—Almost any writing utensil can hide drugs or even weapons. Students can replace the lead or ink with drugs or a weapon. For instance, sewing needles and small knives can be hidden in ergonomic pens, because of their larger bodies.

- *Lipsticks*—The cap of a lipstick makes a good hiding place.
- *Shoes*—The soles and insides of shoes are easy places to conceal something.
- *Clothes*—The baggier the clothes, the better to hide things. Also, some shirts and tops may have pouches, pockets, or gathered material, which make great hiding places.
- *Eyelids*—With fake eyelashes and the bejeweled look currently popular, gluing pills on the lashes or around the eye area may be easily done.
- *Jewelry*—Especially lockets and bracelets (the clasp and the charms) have plenty of room to store items.
- *Fingernails*—Drugs can be hidden underneath a fingernail, and pills can be made into decorative "jewels" on top of the nail.
- *Makeup compacts*—Drugs and small weapons can be stored underneath the powder and inside a makeup sponge.
- *Book spines*—Knives and shanks can be easily hidden in book spines. Ask students to open their books and shake out the pages. As they do so, the spine will open for you to see if anything is tucked inside it.
- *Edges of lockers*— Razors, knives, and other kinds of weapons can easily be stored on the walls and edges of a locker. When searching a locker, always allow the student to run his or her fingers on the walls and edges of the locker. If a student refuses to do so, then you'll know that a prohibited item may be hidden there. Also, hit the walls of the locker to see if they have been removed to store items. Some students are able to manipulate a locker wall by bending the corner or increasing the space between two locker walls that meet.
- *Vehicles*—Vehicles contain numerous hiding places, such as tires, steering wheels, seats, under the hood, behind the stereo, in the spare tire, and so on.

A final note on searches: You *do not* need a parent's permission to search a student and seize contraband. Follow your school board's policies, and do what is necessary to find weapons or drugs. Then contact the parent.

- After you search Burris, remind him why the search was done, never mentioning the name of the student who gave the tip. If you search a student and don't find anything on the student or in the student's locker or car, remind him or her that weapons are prohibited and the consequences are severe. With the student present, call the parent to explain that a search was performed and that nothing was seized. Be explicit when informing the parent that an allegation of a prohibited item in the student's possession was made, and the search was necessary because the allegation had merit. Tell the parent what the SCOC states about weapons and consequences, and remind the parent that maintaining safety, security, and order on campus is the purpose of the SCOC.

If you do seize a weapon, and if possessing it is a penal code violation (for instance, if the weapon is a double-edged knife or a knife with a blade that is 5½ inches or more in length), then the student will be arrested. If the SRO is present, he or she will take over and place the student under arrest. If no SRO is present, then you will need to contact the SRO and ask him or her to come to your campus to make the arrest. Check your state's laws for the age at which a student can be arrested. In Texas, for example, students may be arrested at age 10 for penal code violations. The arresting officer will call the parent and will follow the policies of the school district or the city police department, which should be very similar, if not the same. You will also call the parent and explain about the tip, the search and seizure, the arrest, and the need to start the hearing process according to the SCOC.

The next steps may differ from state to state, but the end result is much the same. If a student violates the SCOC, many consequences may be enforced, such as ISS and OSS, which are the most common. But when an expellable or severe violation occurs, a hearing process will be the norm. Follow what your school board has established, and use the steps below as a guide for a student in general education.

1. When a student is arrested for a penal code violation, the SRO or attending police officer will file paperwork on the incident and will follow the policies set forth by the school district or city police department.

2. You will follow the administrative policies established by the school board. You will notify your principal and/or the area or regional superintendent and then the student's parents. When you contact everyone, be concise yet specific in detail, and relay what your recommendation will be for disciplining the student, which is placement in a disciplinary alternative education program, or DAEP.

3. Set a campus-level conference with the student, the parents, the principal or designated campus hearing officer, the arresting police of-

ficer, and any other person who can provide evidentiary statements that support your recommendation for alternative placement. In many states, you have three to five days to schedule this meeting. If the parents are unable to attend, let them know what will be discussed, what your recommendation is, and then set the meeting. The student may not be available, unless he or she has been released from jail on bail. If the student's parents are available to attend and ask to bring a pastor, a friend, or any other supporter with them, honor that request.

If the parents want to bring a lawyer, they must notify you immediately, so that you will have time to contact your supervisor, who in turn will contact the district's lawyer if needed. *Be sure to follow school district policies when seeking guidance from the district's lawyer.* Your district will be charged a fee each time the lawyer is contacted; hence, usually only certain persons at the district central office are designated to contact the lawyer. Rarely, if ever, do campus administrators have this designation.

If the parents show up for the conference with a lawyer but failed to give you advance notice that the lawyer would be coming, you may do one of two things: either reschedule the meeting so that you have time to obtain legal advice, or proceed with the meeting but ask the lawyer to wait outside until it is complete.

4. Before the conference, assemble a file that includes the student's discipline history, grades, and attendance records, along with statements from students and teachers, and anything else that will support your recommendation that the student be placed in a DAEP. Make copies of the file so that you can distribute them to the principal, the student and parents, and any other appropriate individuals who may need a copy.

5. The principal/campus hearing officer will start the meeting by asking you why you called the meeting. Respond by presenting the information in the file. Start with the most recent SCOC violation, but if the student has committed other SCOC violations in the past, review them in order of occurrence until you reach the present violation and the reason it necessitated a campus hearing. Then review the student's grades, attendance, and any other information you've included in the file to support your recommendation.

6. The student and the parents must be given a chance to respond to the information in the file. If any of them are unable to be present, they may give their input in writing or verbally (e.g., through the phone call when the administrator set the time for the hearing) to be conveyed to the principal/hearing officer. As time allows, other persons present may be given a chance to respond. After everyone has spoken, the

principal will fill out paperwork that states what your recommendation is, and both the student and the parents will sign the document to indicate that they had an opportunity to speak, whether they agree with the recommendation or not. If the parent and student are not present, then the principal will write that fact and why they were unable to sign the document. If the parent gave their input over the phone or in a letter, the principal may write this fact on the document and attach the letter.

7. Based on the information presented at the conference, the principal/hearing officer will either support your recommendation or deny it. If it is denied, then the principal will describe any stipulations that may be attached to the denial, such as having a behavior intervention plan put in place. If the principal supports your recommendation, then a district-level hearing will usually be set.

The campus-level hearing is a due process hearing, where all those attending are allowed to give input regarding the situation. In smaller districts, this is the only hearing that occurs, and the decision made at this hearing is final. In larger districts, once a campus hearing has been completed, a district-level hearing is then convened, as further due process.

At the district hearing, the same procedure will be followed, with the hearing officer making the final decision. The district hearing officer, usually a retired principal or a lawyer, is impartial and acts as a judge who listens to all sides and, based on the data provided, makes a recommendation.

A district hearing is conducted in the same way as the campus-level meeting; you will distribute copies of the student's file to those attending, review the information in the file, and present your recommendation. The student, the parents, and, as appropriate, any others at the meeting will have a chance to speak, and then the district hearing officer will either support your recommendation or deny it. If your recommendation is denied, then the student will be sent back to your campus, but the hearing officer will often apply some stipulations to the student's return, such as the implementation of a BIP.

If the district hearing officer supports your recommendation for the student, then the following will occur.

- The hearing officer will tell everyone how many days the student must stay in the DAEP.

- The hearing officer will tell the student and the parents that the student will have to withdraw from his or her home campus and enroll in the alternative campus.

- The student and the parents will be given a packet that explains the rules and policies of the alternative campus. In some alternative programs, students must wear a uniform and must submit to body searches.

- The student will sign a no-trespassing document acknowledging that he or she will be arrested for setting foot on any school district property during this alternative placement.

- The hearing officer will tell the student that if he or she refuses to attend the DAEP or withdraws from the school district, the time in the DAEP will not start and will resume only if and when the student returns to the district. If the student plans to enroll elsewhere, the receiving school district may follow your district hearing officer's decision by placing the student in its own DAEP.

If a student is arrested and stays in jail, you might not see him for a long while. Regardless, you must follow through with the administrative campus and district hearings in case the student is sent back to your campus sooner than you expected. Even if for some reason the charges are dropped and the district attorney does not pursue a conviction for the violation of the penal code, you still must hold the hearings if that is what your SCOC stipulates. If you don't follow through with the campus and district hearings in a timely manner, then you must allow the student to remain on your campus until he or she violates the SCOC again.

For a student who is in special education, the above process starts differently. First, a manifestation determination (MD) or "link" (connection) individualized education program (IEP) meeting must take place. "MD" and "link" are synonymous in this context: was the student's disability manifested in or linked to the student's behavior? For example, a student is diagnosed as a learning disabled (LD) student in math, and during his English class he gets up and yells profanity. The IEP team would determine if the student's LD in math (the disability) manifested itself in or was linked to the yelling of profanity (the behavior). This meeting might be attended by the same people invited to a campus-level hearing, and it may precede the hearing. However, a special education teacher, a general education teacher, and a diagnostician or assessment person must be invited. At this meeting, two questions will be asked:

1. Was the conduct in question the direct result of the local educational agency's failure to implement the IEP?

2. Was the conduct in question caused by, or did it have a direct and substantial relationship to, the child's disability?

The first question refers to you, your staff, and the rest of the administration. Its purpose is to discover whether the IEP was appropriately put into practice and whether all educators are following the IEP. The second question essentially asks if there is a link between the student's disability and the infraction. If the committee agrees that the school properly implemented the IEP and that the behavior was not linked to the student's disability, then the

MD/link IEP meeting ends and the committee continues with the campus- and district-level hearing process, which is the same as that for a student in general education.

If a link is found between a student's disability and the infraction, the MD/link IEP meeting ends, and the disciplinary hearing begins. During this hearing, alternative disciplinary consequences should be discussed; depending on the severity of the infraction, however, a student may still be sent to DAEP. For example, if a student has an emotional disability, his or her special education file will contain a psychological report. If this report states that the student is impulsive, hates authority figures, angers quickly, and has a fascination with knives, then a link may be found if the student impulsively tried to stab a teacher with a knife, because the disability was manifested in the behavior (impulsivity, quick to anger, brought knife to school). The committee may pursue one of two avenues. First, it can decide that because a link was found, the student will have a behavior intervention plan, or BIP, put into place, or if the student already has a BIP, then it will be reviewed and modified. The student may even be placed in a behavior management classroom full-time and may have some privileges taken away. This pathway is an option if the student's behavior is not penal code violation. So, if the student was impulsive, quick to anger, and brought a butter knife to school, then this might be a good avenue to take.

If the student brought a butcher knife to school and was arrested, then a link may still be found, which means that he *might* be allowed to stay on campus. For example, if a student in first grade has the disability of ED and brought a butcher knife to school, those at the discipline hearing could agree that the student should be placed in a behavior management classroom with loss of privileges and counseling. For an eighth grader who has a history of fantasizing about using knives to kill animals and people, the committee can agree to send the student to a DAEP even though a link has been found. Thus, the finding of a link does not mean a student must stay on your campus. Especially if the student is arrested for a penal code violation, you will proceed with the MD/link IEP meeting and the campus- and district-level hearings, and the student will be placed in a DAEP, a JJAEP, or jail. The IEP committee can agree that even when a link is determined, the best placement for a student is in a DAEP.

Furthermore, federal law pertaining to students with disabilities must be followed [34 CFR 300.530(g)(1)–(3)] [20 USC 1415(k)(1)(G)(i)–(iii)]:

> School personnel may remove a student to an interim alternative educational setting for not more than 45 school days without regard to whether the behavior is determined to

be a manifestation of the child's disability, if the child: (1) carries a weapon to or possesses a weapon at school, on school premises, or to or at a school function under the jurisdiction of a State educational agency (SEA) or a local educational agency (LEA); (2) knowingly possesses or uses illegal drugs, or sells or solicits the sale of a controlled substance, while at school, on school premises, or to or at a school function under the jurisdiction of an SEA or an LEA; or, (3) has inflicted serious bodily injury upon another person while at school, on school premises, or at a school function under the jurisdiction of an SEA or an LEA.

For more information on the specifics of special education and the federal law (IDEA) that delineates how to successfully implement a special education program on your campus, visit http://idea.ed.gov/explore/home.

When handling discipline of students in special education, remember that although IDEA is powerful and provides a basis for some parents to be litigious, IDEA clearly states that students in special education will adhere to the SCOC that all other students in general education must follow. A BIP, for instance, may supplement the SCOC, but it may *never* supplant it. Simply put, all students in special education must follow the SCOC and may be disciplined accordingly when they violate it.

Some Final Considerations about Disciplining Students

Discipline issues with students occur not only on campus but off campus too. Issues will arise on the bus, on field trips, at out-of-town games, and at other school functions. No matter the venue, at all school-sponsored events, you have jurisdiction over your students, and your SCOC can be enforced. Even when a student is not at a school event but commits a penal code violation, the student may still be disciplined per the SCOC. Certain circumstances, like events that take place in a private home (underage drinking), will prevent you from enforcing the SCOC, but in such cases, other means of discipline may be used.

Referrals

You must explain to all teachers and other personnel, including bus drivers, how you would like referrals to be completed and how you will address them. Reiterate that the referral process should be the last step in disciplining students, and that calling parents and handling disciplinary situations in the classroom or on the bus is always preferable. However, for expellable and severe infractions, a referral becomes necessary immediately.

Show your staff how you expect referral paperwork to be filled out, and emphasize the importance of writing down exactly what has occurred. For example, if a student shouts, "I hate you, you stupid cow!" while also punching another student in the face, then that is what must be written:

> *Student A shouted to another student, "I hate you, you stupid cow!" while also punching the student in the face.*

Sometimes staff members misguidedly fail to write down the exact details of an incident, and the lack of details hinders an administrator in upholding the SCOC. For example, you most likely will not act on a referral that states:

> *Student A shouted some mean things to another student, and then she hit the student.*

The above statement is vague and does not help you understand what type of infraction actually occurred. Additionally, you may have a difficulty trying to figure out if the SCOC was violated.

Ask your staff to help you help them by providing every fact and detail that has occurred, so that when you meet with the student and eventually with the parent, you will have as many facts on hand as possible. Explain to your staff that no emotions are allowed on a referral form, and that writing excerpts or using terms from the SCOC will strengthen the referral. For example:

> *Student A verbally and physically assaulted another student by calling her a "fat cow" and punching her right cheek while wearing a large ring on her finger.*

Using the SCOC language—such as "verbally and physically assaulted" in the above example—will help everyone stay true to the intent of school, district, and state disciplinary policies.

Advise teachers not to write "bubble gum" referrals. These are referrals for student behavior that the teachers should be able to handle. Some examples of bubble gum referrals are sending a student to the office for chewing gum in class, for cheating, or for not turning in homework. These kinds of referrals need to be handled in the classroom, by the teacher. If a teacher refers a student to you for such behavior, you may talk to the student, give him or her a warning, and then send the student back to class. Whatever you do, never tell the student that the referral is a waste of your time and that you won't deal with it. Later, go to the teacher and explain why you won't process bubble gum referrals and how teachers must not give their power and authority away by referring students to you for behavior that the teachers could have settled in class.

Discipline on School Buses

The school bus is an extension of the classroom; therefore, discipline on the bus should be handled as it is on campus. Furthermore, bus stops may also be considered extensions of the classroom, and the SCOC may reach these areas as well. Always support your bus drivers, who have a very difficult job:

keeping students safe while driving. Many buses have cameras mounted above the driver's seat. Review recordings from these cameras to support bus drivers and students who have had an issue on the bus. Regularly get on the buses yourself before they depart, know which students ride which bus, and ride the buses sporadically to observe both the students and the driver.

Off-Campus Discipline Issues

When a disciplinary problem takes place off campus, the facts become extremely important. For example, if a student with a high alcohol level was involved in a hit-and-run over the weekend and was arrested, you can follow up by completing administrative paperwork and recommending placement in a DAEP, which means that you will follow through with campus- and district-level hearings. Even if charges against the student are dropped, you can pursue the hearing process. Regardless of whether you decide hearings are appropriate or not, either your SRO or the school district police department can obtain the information you need about the arrest and alleged crime in order to prepare your administrative paperwork.

If a discipline issue occurs but the police are not involved, then disciplining the student may prove more difficult. For example, a parent allows her daughter, who is a cheerleader, to invite all of the cheerleaders and football players to her house on a Saturday night for a party. During the party, the parent allows alcohol to be served and supplies condoms. Many students end up drunk and copulate by the end of the night. On Monday, you receive several calls from parents of children who were at the party, and they want the mother and the daughter who gave the party to be disciplined. Additionally, some cheerleaders and football players also come to you to report what happened at the party, even providing pictures and videos of drunk students. What can you do?

Well, the answer is, not much. If a drunken party occurred at a private house and no police officers were called during the party, then you have no jurisdiction over the students and the SCOC has not been violated. However, in many schools, students who participate in extracurricular activities, along with their parents, are expected to sign a contract, constitution, or the like that details what kinds of behaviors are expected and how demerits or merits will be earned. Through such signed agreements, discipline can occur, and the teacher or coach may assign demerits and kick students off a team, as necessary.

■ ■ ■

Read, review, understand, and employ the SCOC at all times. Always follow what your school board has approved and implemented, and use its language to support your efforts in disciplining. Take the time to teach and reteach exactly what you expect from your staff when following and upholding the

SCOC, and always be fair and consistent. No matter what, always review the school district's policies, procedures, codes, and bylaws that affect your leadership and your campus.

Numerous national and state organizations provide information on both school safety and SRO programs. See "References and Recommended Resources" at the end of this book for examples of resources that can be helpful in establishing the right safety program for your campus.

CHAPTER 8

Handling Crises and Implementing Crisis Plans

Crises and tragedies will happen on your campus, because life happens on school campuses. When they occur, you will help your campus get through them. As with school safety, there are no guarantees that crises can be prevented. What you can guarantee is that a plan or plans to address crises will be created, implemented, practiced, evaluated, and revised.

Elements of a Crisis Plan

The three elements of a crisis plan are *preparation*, *awareness*, and *enforcement*, and they should always be in the minds of administrators and their staff. First, *be prepared*. Have crisis plans in place, and practice them often. Communicate these plans to your staff, students, parents, and central office. Place documents outlining and describing the steps of each plan into a single binder, and make a binder for each staff member on your campus. When practicing these plans, work with the teachers so that they know how to implement each plan.

Second, *be aware* of all that occurs on your campus. As much as possible, be aware of who is on your campus and why, know what activities teachers are doing that take them outside the classroom, and know which areas of your campus are the busiest and most susceptible to violations of the Student Code of Conduct (SCOC). You will need to rely on your staff to help you be knowledgeable of who is where and who is doing what, so teach them to be aware of what occurs on campus. Remind your staff to be vigilant and to report any behavioral changes in students, parents, volunteers, or colleagues and any rumored fights or potentially tragic events that might be avoidable.

Third, *enforce* all rules, policies, and crisis plans consistently and continuously. Expect all staff members to do the same and to collaborate on what enforcement should look like, so that everyone is enforcing uniformly. If your campus earns a reputation for not enforcing its rules, policies, and crisis plans, then violating them becomes easier.

How to Create a Crisis Plan

When you are creating a crisis plan, it is important to remind yourself that you are a part of a human organization. Human behavior is unpredictable and may not be optimal during a crisis. Thus, no matter how perfect a crisis plan seems, it will not be foolproof.

Unfortunately, numerous tragedies have occurred at schools in recent years. News stories about such incidents usually prompt school districts to evaluate and revise their current crisis plans or to create new ones. Review your current crisis plans and decide if they need to be revamped. Follow the steps outlined below to prepare for possible crises. Some of these steps may be performed simultaneously, as needed.

A. ***Identify.*** Recognize what your campus's needs are and what kinds of calamities are possible. All campuses should prepare for bad weather (e.g., tornadoes, hurricanes, blizzards, floods) and other crises, including the following:

- Fire
- Chemical spill
- Hostage situation
- Kidnapping
- Sexual assault
- Death
- Bomb threat
- Active shooter

B. ***Create the plan.*** Having a crisis plan coordinator on campus is a good idea. This person could be a teacher, but a member of the administrative team would be more appropriate. A crisis team should also be assembled, consisting of five to seven people who will discuss and approve all crisis plans and procedures. The coordinator, with guidance from the crisis team, would help create the assorted plans for the campus to follow. An administrator must be on the team, but it should be the team as a whole that agrees on the need for a crisis plan and when and how to develop it.

Each crisis plan should have a list of procedures that is easy to check, and the administration should follow the same checklist. Use the checklist below as a guide or template for creating and implementing useful and well-organized plans.

1. *Identify the crisis and the appropriate crisis plan, and put the plan into action.*

2. *Contact those who are in immediate danger, and signal to them that you are in crisis plan mode.* The signal could be a code word for a hostage situation, for example, or a series of bells rung for a fire drill. If a crisis has occurred off campus, using a developed phone tree to notify all staff will help expedite the dissemination of information.

3. *Shut or lock all doors, as needed. If the crisis involves a shooter or hostages, the crisis team should work with the teachers to find the safest place to hide until help arrives.* Hiding places might be a closet or a bathroom, under desks, or in corners of a classroom. If teachers have windows in their classrooms, then closing the curtains or shades may need to be a part of this process.

4. *Determine who should call 911 and then the central office.* At least three people should be designated to call 911, and they should know what specific details should be given to the dispatcher. This may seem obvious, but an infamous Texas case provides an example of why designees should be named to call 911. At a time when trained special education teachers were legally allowed to restrain students and drop them to the floor, a teacher, without malice, restrained a seventh grader to the floor. She lay across the student's back, as she had been taught. Within moments, the student stopped struggling and quit breathing. Immediately the assistant principal and the school nurse were called to the room. Knowing that the student needed to be taken to the hospital, the educators agreed that 911 should be called. However, the despotic principal made it clear that only she was allowed to call 911. Since the principal was off campus, the educators were uncertain of what to do. Tragically, the student died, because the assistant principal called 911 too late. Having more than one designee to call 911 will possibly save a life. Fortunately, restraining

students on the floor is no longer done and many school districts have their educators complete a program that focuses on specialized restraints, like the Crisis Prevention Institute's program.

5. ***Determine whether everyone is safe***. Walking around the campus and checking each room, calling into each room, and talking to each staff member—or any other means of finding out if everyone is safe—is to be done ASAP. Throughout a crisis, the crisis team can call staff using a developed phone tree, so that each person on staff will know to expect a call from a certain crisis team member. However, explain to the staff that, depending on the situation, another person might call, like a police officer. Have a code word prepared for the officer to give to the staff, so that they will know for sure that they are no longer in danger. If someone is hurt or is not accounted for, a designated crisis team member will record those names and injuries, so that help from the staff or the police and medical personnel can be dispatched.

   The crisis team also needs to determine how students and staff will be kept safe if a crisis occurs during a passing period or lunchtime and how all staff and students will be accounted for. Look for areas such as closets, bathrooms, classrooms, and any other places where students can take cover during non-instructional time. If possible, have teachers check the hallways for stray students and faculty before closing and locking their classroom doors.

6. ***Have crisis bags ready.*** The crisis team at one very proactive school bought a backpack for each classroom and office on campus. Each backpack contained a first aid kit, two bottles of water, and class and/or staff rosters, with emergency contact names and phone numbers. This bag was to be updated and checked after each practice of a crisis plan and when a new student or staff member joined the campus. These crisis bags helped make accounting for everyone a bit easier. In the bag for the front/main office, be sure to include a roster that shows all staff and students for the entire school and their emergency contacts and phone numbers, plus the phone numbers of the central office. During a crisis, have the front office secretaries take with them the updated registration cards along with their backpack of emergency items, such as hard copies of school, student, and staff information and an electronic notebook that includes all sensitive information (e.g., medical needs for dia-

betic students and staff) to whatever secure place that they go to. This will provide both a nontechnological and a technological way to reach the parents once everyone is outside or when students need to be taken to another location to be reunited with their parents.

C. *Implement and practice!* To ensure that all staff and students know what to do when a crisis plan is in action, lots of practice must be done throughout the year. Check with your school district's policies and city and state codes for their requirements about how many times a crisis plan must be practiced. For example, some city fire departments expect fire drills to be performed four times a school year. At the beginning of the year, information should be sent home to parents alerting them of the crisis plans that will be implemented and practiced throughout the year. When a practice or real event occurs and a crisis plan is implemented, your school should inform parents of what occurred and why the crisis plan needed to be activated.

   All plans may be practiced sequentially on the same day. For example, one school decided to follow its fire drills with practice of all other crisis plans so that the students and teachers would be familiar with the types of possible crises and the action plan for each.

D. *Evaluate, revise, reteach, and redistribute all crisis plans.* After each practice and real crisis plan implementation, the procedures should be evaluated, revised, retaught, and redistributed, as needed. The crisis team is charged with this task, which includes contacting the school district's police department, the city police department, and the local fire department for tips, and implementing their suggestions after a crisis has occurred. In some school districts, a school district police department is established. In others, a city or county police department is partnered with the school district in providing police officers or school resource officers on campuses. In either case, working with the police department and gaining its insight on how to strengthen a crisis plan are necessary. After a real crisis, you and the crisis team will have to debrief the incident with the district's central office and the police and fire departments, as appropriate.

E. *Provide counseling after a crisis.* The crisis team should identify counselors throughout the school district who will be able to provide their services to staff, students, and family members after a real crisis has occurred. In some cities, private therapists, counselors, psychologists, and psychiatrists will donate their time to schools that need counseling services. A reminder about counselors: They should never be put in the position of being disciplinarians, because after a crisis, both students and parents should feel comfortable going to someone who has not disciplined those students. Students need to have safe places to go on a campus, and counselors should provide that haven.

The steps above can be tailored to your campus's needs. If you are a new administrator on a campus, look for the current crisis plans and review them with your crisis team to see whether they could be improved. Remember, all staff on your campus should know how to be prepared, to be aware, and to enforce the crisis plans, so that tragedies can be avoided whenever possible. Finally, learn from others' tragedies and employ safety measures to help keep your campus whole.

The Current State of Affairs

Many heartbreaking incidents that have happened throughout our nation in recent years highlight the current state of affairs in our society and on our school campuses. These tragedies are sometimes horrific and therefore are difficult to ponder, but they nevertheless provide crisis teams with a point of reference for discussing the types of crises that could occur in their communities. Even when such incidents do not take place on a campus, the aftermath still can affect those on a campus. As you read through this next section, think about all that needs to be done to keep your campus safe from harm. It may be an impossible task, but one that you and your crisis team must constantly address to the best of your abilities.

Sexual Assaults

Sexual assault is a statutory offense that involves any type of physical sexual contact without consent. It can be characterized as a rape, groping, sexual penetration, lewd contact, and indecent exposure. At one time, reports of sexual assaults were generally localized to the high school level, but as years passed, they became more frequent in middle schools and then at the elementary level. In some cases, administrators and educators act swiftly to stop potential sexual assaults on campuses, but at other times, administrators and educators are not told early enough to intervene or they do little to stop penal code violations.

At the high school level, date rapes and other forms of dating violence are being reported again and again. Both male and female students have become obsessed with another student or an educator to the point of stalking them and threatening to kill them. Others are boldly behaving in ways that are socially unacceptable and criminal. At one high school, a group of football players were known as the "Gropers." The Gropers brazenly touched girls' breasts and buttocks with impunity. Sometimes the Gropers would surround a female student and take turns gyrating on her while they laughed and hollered. Although the administration had received many student and staff reports about these actions, it did little to stop them. One day the Gropers cornered two female students with the intention of gang-raping them. They were stopped before penetration occurred, but the girls' clothes were ripped from their bodies, and their sense of security and trust was stripped from them as well. In this case, unchecked male students were allowed to sexually assault female students at will without intervention by the administration. When the administrators did finally intervene, they had no documentation to prove that they had acted responsibly by investigating and stopping the sexual assault. The lesson to be learned from this example is you must always enforce all rules at all times equally among the student population. By doing the right thing and seeking to protect all students on your campus from harm, you can avoid being the administrator who is disgraced on the nightly news.

At an elementary school in Arkansas, a third grader was released to an unknown male visitor three times over a four-month period. No one asked for the man's driver's license or any other form of ID, and no one checked the child's records to make sure that the visitor was on the list of persons to whom the child could be released. Each time the visitor picked up the girl from school, he took her to his home, raped her, and then brought her back to school on the same day. The campus staff members who released the girl to the pedophile did not do so maliciously, and they probably never fathomed that the child was being raped repeatedly. However, because of their inappropriate actions and lack of diligence, the parents sued the school board, the principal, and every person who allowed the child to leave the campus with the pedophile. The lesson here is to know the persons to whom you are releasing your students or with whom your students choose to leave campus, and absolutely know who the sexual offenders are in the area around your school.

Unfortunately, numerous incidents in which teachers have sexually assaulted students have been reported. Many states have addressed these sexual assaults by adding statutes in both their education and penal codes that specifically address teachers who sexually assault students. Even if the student is of age to give consent, the teacher may face criminal charges and sanctions per the education and penal codes if he or she has a sexual affair with a student. Explaining this to teachers at the start of every school year and as needed throughout the year will hopefully prevent any of your teachers from sexually assaulting a student. It is wise to document your communications to teachers about this subject.

Additional situations you must be prepared for include sexual assault of teachers by students and/or false student reports of teachers making sexual advances on students. Some students who behave in this manner either do not understand or do not care that a teacher's livelihood and reputation are at stake and that rumors of sexual misconduct can even lead to legal proceedings against a teacher. You must ensure that students, parents, and staff are thoroughly informed about the dangers and consequences of false and fabricated stories. Showing them the state codes that spell out what sexual assault and false accusations look like could help deter malicious behavior. Examples of codes that address sexual assaults can be found in appendix C.

School Stabbings and Shootings

How do administrators prevent a stabbing or a shooting on a campus? Some may say that the answer is obvious and simple and that stabbing and shooting incidents will happen only on campuses whose administrators aren't *prepared*, *aware*, and *enforcing* all rules. However, think about the following incident and what the educators at that high school may have felt when a stabbing occurred so quickly and without warning.

A young female student broke up with her longtime boyfriend. The boyfriend begged her not to leave him, but she no longer wanted to be with a boy who didn't respect her. The boy was distraught and angry and told her that if he couldn't have her, no one else would either. The next day, during a morning passing period in a school of more than 2,000 students, the boy walked up to the girl and slit her throat with a knife. The halls were full of students and educators, but no one realized what the boy was about to do. After the incident, no notes, text messages, or the like were found that pointed to the boy's plan to kill the girl. However, during the days leading up to the murder, friends of both the boy and the girl were witnesses to his rants about killing her and himself if she would no longer be his girlfriend. He hid the knife as he approached her, and his friends didn't think he would ever try to kill his own girlfriend, especially in front of so many people. So how can administrators and other educators prevent these kinds of violent acts? The answer is that sometimes they can't.

Another example occurred at a California elementary school. The principal was shot to death by a janitor who was upset after his employment was terminated. No one had suspected that the janitor would harm the principal. No one saw a gun when the janitor entered the school and went to the principal's office, and once the gun was brandished, there was no chance for the principal or anyone else to stop him.

When a disturbed person has an agenda and is determined to fulfill it, there is little that can be done to prevent a fatal incident unless someone has an idea beforehand of what may occur. Administrators and educators must understand that they may not be able to prevent acts of violence on campus. You and your colleagues must always be on guard, however, and must take any potential warning signs seriously. In addition, students must be encouraged to report threats made by other students. Protect those on your campus by all means necessary, which means calling for help and following school board policy. If you feel that a tragedy is imminent, call your SRO (school resource officer) or the city police and keep tabs on the whereabouts and actions of the person in question until help arrives.

Bullying

Much information is available on bullying and the various ways a bully can reach a victim. In fact, many state education and penal codes address exactly what educators should do when confronted with information about a bully. These codes also spell out preventive actions that can be put in place, as well as steps for implementing character education.

Bullies work at hurting another person physically and emotionally, through actions, texts, emails, social media, and phone calls. They may befriend others only to ridicule them later. Altered or unflattering pictures may be taken and then posted online or sent to people at a school. Groups of students may be bullies, taunting one student at a time, sexually, physically, and verbally assaulting him or her daily. In some cases, they may constantly seek to harm other students "just because," as in the case of the young Irish immigrant who hanged herself because a group of students continuously bullied and sexually assaulted her and she felt she had no other recourse but to commit suicide.

Bullying is harmful, and sometimes the victim becomes an unwilling perpetrator. Often a bullied victim brings a knife or gun to school in order to stop a bully, and the bullied victim becomes the punished one because of the weapon. Some perpetrators, such as the Columbine shooters, have been bullied and believe that the only way to stop the bullying is to kill. To help prevent a bullied victim from bringing a weapon to school, clear procedures of how a student who is being bullied can seek help on campus should be foremost. Daily announcements, posters, and any other kinds of communication to help students feel safe about reporting bullying must be provided in schools to end bodily harm and weapons on campus.

Stopping bullies may not be entirely possible, but a student's feelings of despair or being trapped can be lessened if administrators are diligent in how they handle this type of situation. Once a bully is identified, be sure that he or she understands the consequences of bullying. Remind all students and staff how to safely report bullying, and emphasize that retaliation on a student or staff member who reports bullying is a serious matter: in some states, retaliation against an employee is a felony. Finally, some schools believe that character education or teaching the Golden Rule helps lessen bullying. Whatever technique is favored on your campus, implement it with fervor and dedication.

Tragedies That Affect Individuals and the Campus

At times, there will be sad events that affect only one student or staff member or that affect the whole campus. There will be deaths throughout a school year that affect an individual on campus: a teacher's father may pass away, or a student's mother may die. Such events can be distressing for the staff members or students involved, and efforts to help them cope with the event must be made.

There will also be deaths that affect the whole campus. With the rise of teen suicides, campuses throughout the nation are facing challenges in helping an entire student body and staff with their grief after a student's suicide. Additionally, car accidents due to drunk driving or inexperienced drivers, kidnappings, and even murder can affect a whole campus. Your crisis plans should include procedures for responding to an unexpected death and steps for encouraging everyone on campus to cope with a death.

Individual and campus tragedies may have positive implications. First, a tragedy may highlight a problem that may not have been known by campus staff or parents, and counseling or other interventions can be employed to help prevent similar events. Second, it may bring the students, parents, and staff closer to each other, possibly building trust and camaraderie. Finally, it will remind you of the delicate nature of adolescence, the possible vulnerabilities of the people on your campus, and the importance of establishing plans that may prevent tragedies, as well as plans for coping with sad events when they do occur.

Community Tragedies

The Texas Luby's massacre, New York's 9/11, the Virginia Tech massacre, the 2013 tornado in Moore, Oklahoma, and the Sandy Hook Elementary School shootings in Connecticut are all examples of community-wide and citywide tragedies. Additionally, some military towns have deployed soldiers in war zones, and when any of those soldiers are killed in action, the whole town mourns them, because everyone understands what being a part of a military family means. Not only do these kinds of events affect those who are personally linked to a tragedy, but those who are indirectly linked will also feel the aftereffects of a community tragedy.

As a school administrator, you may ask yourself, "Since I am assigned to lead a campus, what are my responsibilities in preventing tragedies within the community and city?" Administrators' arms reach well past the school building. For example, a principal at an elementary school periodically read stories to the students during their lunchtime. These stories were based on character and safety education, specifically on being aware of your surroundings and of others' actions. One of the stories involved the recognition of strangers and the actions to take if one feels threatened. During the year, a first grader was walking home with her friends when a car pulled up to the group. The driver offered a ride to the whole group, even promising ice cream cones. The first grader told her friends to ignore the stranger, to run to the nearest home, and to keep ringing the doorbell until someone answered. When she said this, the driver sped off. The principal's seemingly innocuous story helped prevent a community tragedy. News of this incident led to similar lunchtime stories being presented in elementary and middle school campuses across that city. Thus, the principal's positive approach affected the whole city by raising awareness of how educators, parents, and community members can help keep students safe.

What Are You to Do?

Do something! No matter what the crisis, the information tips you receive, or the gut feeling you have, do something in response to help prevent harm to others on your campus. Ask questions, seek new information, find supporting evidence, and if something doesn't feel right, then find out why. Do not make the mistake of taking no action.

Doing something means investigating, documenting, allowing due process to occur, and reporting to the police and district central office any disconcerting information. When a person whom you and your staff have never seen before comes on campus and wants to sign out a student, ask that person a series of questions, and call the child's parent to gain permission. Don't be timid because you feel that your asking may hurt someone's feelings. Hurting someone's feelings should be secondary to keeping all those in your care safe—always.

Your inaction could potentially lead to a tragedy like the one at a high school campus where two police officers arrested a student. Hours later, the student's body was found in a ditch; he had been shot to death. It was later discovered that the two "police officers" were gang members dressed in police uniforms, and they murdered the student. In another incident, a gang member snuck onto a middle school campus, hid in the bathroom, and waited for students to come in so that he could give them drugs and recruit them to be drug mules. Some young-looking adults can appear to be students and are able to walk on a campus undetected. That is one reason why you must know each child and staff member who belongs on your campus, by using ID badges or some other form of identification to recognize your students and staff.

■ ■ ■

Protect yourself and those on your campus by *doing something!* Investigate, document, allow due process, and report to authorities. You can't prevent every wicked idea and action that may occur on your campus, but ensuring that your staff are *prepared, aware,* and *enforcing* the rules and expectations of the campus will no doubt prevent some tragedies. For links to helpful websites that will help you prepare for crises, see "References and Recommended Resources" at the end of this book.

CHAPTER 9

Parting Advice

The following advice is based on years of experience and knowledge acquired on the job and summarizes some of the points covered in earlier chapters. You may not be able to tackle these suggestions all at once, but review them periodically to see if something new strikes you that could help you become a better, more successful leader.

Be Your Best!

Strive to be your best by demonstrating through your performance on the job that you deserve the position that you have earned. Start by reading everything that pertains to your campus, such as policies and instructional programs and anything else that influences the successes of all at your school. Know what your campus improvement plan states and follow its objectives and goals, keeping your campus in line with them. Be your best by always seeking to learn how to perform your job better.

Live Your Educational Philosophy

Believe in your own philosophy, and figure out how it aligns with the campus and district visions, missions, goals, and objectives. Live your philosophy, especially if you feel strongly about it and if it provides the basis for your moral convictions. Understand, however, that your philosophy may change as you gain experience and knowledge about leading a campus, so always remain open to new ideas.

Don't Be a Know-it-all, Because You Don't Know It All

In a new position, there are always new things to learn, so listen to those who try to help you strengthen your campus. Unless you are joining a brand-new or reorganized campus, many of the staff will have been on the campus longer than you and will have valuable information that may help you in your role as administrator, so listen, listen, and listen! It's okay that you don't know everything. You can't and won't know everything, but be sure that you know where you can find the answers you need. This is why getting to know those gurus on your campus and at the central office is so important: they will help you find those answers.

Admit When You Are Wrong

No one is ever right all of the time. If you are wrong in a situation, own up to it, apologize, and correct the situation, if possible. Let others see that you are human and are able to learn from your mistakes and do the right thing. Practice humility.

Don't Look for Reasons to Be Offended

Although you have earned a position at a campus, the culture of the community may be unfamiliar to you or even the antithesis of what you know. One assistant principal (AP), for example, moved from the western to the eastern part of the United States and found herself being asked, "What are you?" The staff, students, and parents were familiar with American Indians and Hispanics of Puerto Rican descent, but not with Hispanics of Mexican descent. Hence, the question was posed to ascertain the AP's ethnicity. She chose not to be offended and instead took the opportunity to educate those who wanted to know about her. Remember that some people are not intending to offend when they are blunt; they just may not know how to communicate tactfully what they want to know.

Additionally, being tolerant when learning about a new environment and culture will help you be accepted, and you can figure out during this time whether this new environment and culture are where you will succeed. Take the opportunity to ask questions about what you need to know, and rephrase questions for others in a more respectful manner, as needed. Be tolerant, but do not forsake yourself by allowing others to take advantage of you. It is one thing to be tolerant, but it is another to be ridiculed and disrespected.

Leave Your Biases and Prejudices at Home

Just because you wouldn't behave as someone else does or you wouldn't wear something that another is person is wearing, that doesn't mean it is wrong. For example, you may have been a very meticulous, reserved, and organized teacher, and you believe that those habits helped your students succeed. Now you find yourself evaluating and appraising a teacher who is disorganized and loud and doesn't follow a lesson plan the way you would, but you discover that her students are successful too. As long as the students are learning and transferring their knowledge, judging the teacher based on how you would teach is unfair and unethical. Instead, assess her performance according to established criteria and how her students respond. Essentially, you are expected to judge the teacher against herself, rather than comparing her to yourself or to anyone else. Be fair to the teachers on your campus, and appreciate them for their unique qualities and instructional techniques. They are individuals with distinct individual strengths.

Take the same approach with the students, parents, and any other person who walks onto your campus. Transferring your biases, frustrations, and prejudices onto another person is unprofessional. Judge a person's actions, not the person. If a student is arrested for selling marijuana on your campus, for example, then address the violation of both the Student Code of Conduct and the penal code, but don't assume that the student is a lost cause. Being objective will help you stay fair, ethical, and professional.

Read All Policies, Procedures, Codes, and Laws That Affect Your Campus

In order to enforce the rules that apply to your campus, you must know what they are and what the consequences are for not following them. A good practice is to highlight, tab, and underline specific policies in each handbook, guidebook, and other resource that helps you perform your job well. For instance, the APs at a high school were all disciplinarians, and they each had a hard copy of the Student Code of Conduct on their desks, highlighted and tabbed so that they could quickly and effortlessly locate information on the rules their students frequently violated. This strategy also helped them find the school board–approved language to include when writing student referrals. At another school, one administrator was assigned to study everything related to the budget, another studied everything concerning special populations, and the third learned all about dealing with the food and health codes. These three administrators then became gurus of the domains that they studied. This strategy made all of their jobs easier, since no one had to learn all of the policies, procedures, codes, and laws concerning each area of the campus.

Understand Immunity

There will be times when a legal matter comes up, and you will need to contact legal representation. Before this occurs, understand what immunities you have as an educator and an administrator. At the federal level, the Fourteenth Amendment and 42 USC 1983 are frequently cited as the basis of lawsuits against schools and educators. Established legal precedent in cases based on these laws is that because educators cannot make policy (school boards do), they cannot be liable at the federal level for school district policies. Hence, you may have immunity at the federal level with regard to some laws. However, other laws, such as IDEA (Individuals with Disabilities Education Act), can apply to anyone who has not properly implemented an individualized education program (IEP).

At the state level, immunity for educators and administrators is usually guaranteed through both education and government codes, but *only* if the educator has performed his or her duties according to the job description and in the course of keeping a safe and orderly learning environment. Immunity becomes null and void if the penal code and/or the government code have been violated. So be aware of what immunities you have in your state.

Allow Colleagues and Students to Ask You Personal Questions

As long as you feel comfortable answering personal questions, then do, conveying what you want others to know and/or enough to answer the question. If you don't feel comfortable answering a particular question, then kindly respond with a polite, "Thank you for that question, but I don't feel comfortable answering," or "That is a good question, but I'm going to choose to not answer it." Additionally, some questions may be posed about your religion, political affiliation, marital status, family status, and other very personal subjects. Again, it is your choice whether or not you answer these questions, but do not take offense. For some people, this is a blunt way to get to know you or to see how you react to certain questions. Keep in mind that whatever you tell someone is likely to be repeated to others, so only say what you don't mind others knowing.

In Challenging Situations, Be Confident and Don't Show Emotion

One principal was accused of being a racist, even though she was of the same race as the accusing student, because the principal had assigned him to an alternative school after he sexually assaulted another student. Hence, the student's name-calling was not personal but was due to that principal's being in a position of authority. When parents find themselves in a school-related situation that they can't win, they sometimes resort to name-calling too. To rise above these situations, project confidence and maintain emotional detachment. Concentrate on conveying the facts of the event, what the SCOC or other handbook states, and follow school board policy. Again, using the precise language that has been approved by the school board will help you in difficult situations.

Remember, It's Not Personal—It's Professional

Sometimes you will have to reprimand, correct, or remind someone who does something that is not aligned with any campus rules and policies. Emotions will run high and feelings may be hurt, so a reminder that your action is professional and not personal may be warranted. In one instance, two parents (from different families) got into a physical altercation with each other on a campus. Although both parents were banned from the campus, one of them insisted that the banning was personal, because she believed the principal didn't like her. The principal had to remind her that the other parent had been banned too and that the reason for the ban was their physical dispute in front of their children and others. The principal also reminded her that the ban would last for a specified period and that if no other violations occurred, they would both be welcomed back on campus. Presenting facts and not emotions helped the principal finally get through to the parent.

Don't Jump to Conclusions

Base your decisions and conclusions on facts and not on emotions. If the data are ambiguous, give each person the benefit of the doubt, but make a professional judgment based on data. Remember to employ due process, gathering everyone's side of a story and investigating further if needed. After you have all the information you need, only then will you issue your decision. Teach everyone on your campus to do the same.

Learn about the Community

Become familiar with the community in which your campus is located. Driving around the neighborhood will give you a feel for the socioeconomic status of your students as well as the types of housing options, parks, student hangouts, and businesses and other institutions in the area. Patronize local stores and restaurants, and stop in and introduce yourself. The owners and managers of some of them may be interested in partnering with your school by donating time, money, and other resources.

Make Visits

Visit churches and other community organizations in which your students participate. When possible, arrange to hold school-related meetings off campus at places throughout the community, like an apartment building, a clubhouse, or a church. Doing this will bring the school to parents who may not have the transportation to visit the school. These visits will also give you visibility, and you'll connect with parents and the community, while learning about the cultural backgrounds of your students.

Home visits may be an excellent practice to adopt too. The week before school started each year, one high school principal loaded the teachers on buses and had them go to every neighborhood that fed into the school. The teachers walked around the neighborhoods, visiting each home, duplex, and apartment that housed a high school student. They introduced themselves to the students, asked them to tell a bit about themselves and their interests and answered any questions the students had. Each student was given a postcard with the school's logo and Web address on it, plus reminders of when school started, the cost of breakfasts and lunches, and dress code expectations. If the student wasn't home, they left the postcard at the door. These home visits were such a success that in subsequent years, juniors and seniors joined the teachers for the visits. Their presence was even more powerful, because they could answer questions from a peer's perspective.

Enforce Policies

Do not set a precedent of allowing students or any other person on campus to get away with violating a rule. If a rule is violated, meet with the rule breaker as soon as possible and explain how you expect things to be done. You may have to model those expectations, and depending on the frequency and/or severity of a violation, you may have to formally reprimand the rule breaker. As you enforce campus and district policies, be consistent and fair, and give due process. When reprimanding a violator, state what rule, policy, or code was violated, the consequences, and your professional judgment based on the facts. Communicating how the process works will help the other person understand your position and action.

Be a Supporter

Support your teachers in what they do, and *let them know* that you support them. Thank them, highlight their successes and those of their students, and brag about them. Recognize your administrative staff as well. Let them know that you value them and that you are happy with their performance, but be specific in your praise. Some principals will give candy bars with a message, or a cute toy that symbolizes something. One principal put a red clown's nose in each teacher's mailbox with the note, "Have a happy day and hug a clown," because during the professional development workshop the previous day, a clown had performed for the staff, reinforcing the motto "Be positive and have a happy day!" Do whatever you can to keep the morale of the campus high and positive.

You Are an Influencer, So Be a Model for Others

If you are following a successful principal, give yourself time to find out how the previous administration did things. All on the campus know that you are now the principal, but they also know if your predecessor left you a squared-away campus, so learn what made it so. You may want to continue many of those practices, at least initially. Model the changes you want to see, but don't try to change everything at once. Gently and in time make the school the way you'd like it to be.

From the beginning, have an open-door policy, so that you and your staff, students, and parents may get to learn about each other. An open-door policy also helps the health of your campus, because it allows everyone to see that you are approachable and not a despot. It will contribute to a familial environment.

Remember, you influence the campus culture, and the campus culture influences you. Be aware of your actions and how they affect your leadership. If you expect punctuality, then be at campus early. If you expect professional communication from your teachers, then communicate with them professionally. Continuously model what school pride looks like. Conversely, be aware of the dynamics and condition of your school, so that you are not negatively affected by its shortcomings. You want to foster a climate and culture that are healthy, productive, and familial, and you will want others on campus to do the same. Model what you expect, and you will influence others to follow your lead.

Mentoring Is Essential

Find a mentor for yourself, if one is not assigned to you, and rely on that person to answer your questions and guide you. In turn, mentor your teachers, especially those whom you evaluate and appraise. First-year teachers must have a mentor and a guide, and sometimes the best person is you. Be prepared to give adequate time to these individuals. Encourage all teachers to become more knowledgeable about their area and discipline, to be leaders, and to pursue higher education. Support those who want to become future administrators.

Mentor students by becoming a club sponsor or a tutor, or teach a course once a semester or when it fits with your schedule. Always be a mentor in some form to a group of students so that you can remind yourself where you came from: teaching students in the classroom. This will help you to continue to understand the students and the teachers.

Know about the Students on Your Campus

What time do students reach the campus in the morning? Where do they go after school? Do they go home to an empty home? Do they have to take care of younger siblings? Which students have a job? Which ones have children and may be married? Is there food at home? Are there accessible drugs at home? Is abuse occurring at home? Are any students caring for a sick family member? If you know about the challenges your students face, you will be better equipped to counsel them when they have problems at school and to support them in their interests and goals.

Always Seek to Improve Yourself

Continue to grow professionally by pursuing professional development. Many states mandate that you earn a certain number of hours in professional development periodically, so find courses or activities that will enhance your knowledge and skills as a leader. For instance, look for professional development on the special programs that are at your campus, on the student discipline issues that may be prevalent at your school, or on crisis planning.

Help Others Succeed

You are responsible for everyone on your campus, so assist others in achieving success. If someone is not successful, then help that person identify and strengthen areas of weakness. For example, when a teacher struggles with delivering instruction to his class, model for him various ways of delivering instruction and engaging students. Allow him to observe other teachers or just talk about his ideas of what he would like to do in order to improve. Do whatever you can to provide opportunities for each person on your campus to flourish. Cultivate leaders, responsible teachers and learners, and a strong community.

Trust and Be Trusted

Trust only those you have vetted, and never speak ill of anyone on campus or within the district. The walls have ears, and gossip and complaints always make it back to the person in question. Many times, an elaborated or much worse version of the gossip is relayed, and that only adds fuel to the fire. Pass along this advice to your teachers, because they will talk about you and you may hear things that are not true about yourself. If this happens, confront the teacher or teachers in a professional manner, and give them a chance to explain. Then, let them know what you feel and what you expect from them. Sometimes, misunderstandings and misperceptions can be cleared up by simply talking.

Discover who you can trust, and be trustworthy yourself. You will need someone to vent to and who can vent to you. Usually, another educational administrator is best, especially one who is in the same position as you, because that person will know exactly what you are going through. Even someone you trust may inadvertently share something you confided, so always be mindful that your words may come back to bite you. It's best to confide only what you don't mind being public.

Trust that your staff will do what you expect, and when they don't, give them the benefit of the doubt until there is no doubt. Let the teachers know what your expectations are, and give them examples. Clearly communicating your goals and expectations increases the chances that they will be met, and it will cultivate a trustful environment.

Your Time Is Yours

When you leave the campus, leave your work behind as well, so that you can enjoy your family and friends, pursue your favorite pastimes, and take care of personal obligations. At times you may have to take work home, but try not to make this a habit. Your job is a 24-hour duty, so don't be surprised if you receive a phone call at three o'clock in the morning, informing you that the school alarm went off and you must meet the police to secure the building. These types of events are unpreventable and will encroach on your personal time, but as much as possible, keep work out of your personal time. Help your teachers to follow your lead, and be careful not to make demands of them that intrude on their personal time.

Conversely, never bring your home life to school. You are a professional and always need to behave as one. Allowing your home life to invade your school life may decrease your professional success and may be seen as a weakness. Once again, encourage your teachers to follow your lead by keeping their personal lives at home. Recognize, however, that some teachers may come to you for personal advice and guidance. If you feel comfortable in a counselor role, then allow teachers to come to you with their troubles, especially when their troubles threaten to affect the learning environment.

Accept that teachers, students, and parents may see you as a person who is all-knowing or at least more knowledgeable about life than they are. Or they may see you as a confidant, likening you to a counselor or therapist. Sometimes you are seen as a person who would hear a confession and hold it confidential. Hence, you may be told things that may embarrass you or that are more than you wanted to know. If you don't want to be in this situation, let the other person know immediately. If you are comfortable hearing confidential information, then do keep it confidential.

Don't Take Things Too Seriously

Learn to laugh at yourself, because if you take yourself too seriously, you won't take pleasure in your position as school administrator. Have fun, learn all that you can, and find the humor in as much of your daily interactions and activities as possible.

■ ■ ■

Enjoy your time as an educational administrator, with all its challenges and rewards. Your leadership will be talked about in years to come, so make your mark a positive and productive one. Love what you do, do it well, and facilitate the success of those on your campus. This is your time to shine!

Appendix A

Guide to Understanding Special Programs

In the chart on the following pages, special programs are grouped according to the types of criteria they require for entry into the program.

1. The Student Must Be Assessed to Qualify for Services, or the Student Must Qualify for Services through Eligibility

Program	Program Definition
Early Childhood (EC)	Early Childhood programs are for children from three to six years old. EC programs focus on the developmental, social, and emotional growth that a child must acquire to be successful in a kindergarten and first grade classroom. Head Start and pre-kindergarten are EC programs.
English as a Second Language (ESL), English Language Learners (ELL), and Migrant	ESL and ELL are programs for students who are learning English as a second language. In this type of program, an English-speaking teacher helps students learn the basic English and language arts skills needed for academic success. Migrant programs focus on helping migrant or transient families stay in a school district long enough for the children to become academically proficient and successful.

Who Qualifies	What Campus Leaders Must Know
Children aged three to six may qualify for this program. In some cases, a child must meet at least one of several specific qualifications, such as the following, in order to enter an EC program. The child must • Have a handicap or disability • Have Limited English Proficiency • Be a military dependent • Be homeless • Have a low socioeconomic status or be classified as poor	Most EC programs are half-day, but some school districts have full-day programs because they choose to spend local money on a full day. EC programs are not usually prerequisites for enrolling in kindergarten or first grade. Hence, some students who do not participate in EC programs may seem unprepared for kindergarten or first grade.
Students who do not speak, write, or read English proficiently qualify for the ESL or ELL program. Many states, school districts, and schools have parents complete a Home Language Survey, which identifies families who speak a language other than English in the home. The survey indicates to the ESL/ELL teacher and coordinator that a student may need specialized courses to learn English. Many states, school districts, and schools have parents complete a Migrant Survey. The survey consists of a series of questions, such as "Do you move frequently because of your job?"	Students who are in an ESL or ELL program can be pulled out of class to receive services. However, some schools have the ESL or ELL teacher go into the regular education classrooms as co-teachers instead. Many immigrants coming from another country qualify for an ESL or ELL program. Therefore, many languages may be represented in a single ESL or ELL classroom. Migrant programs focus on helping students who come from migrant or transient families gain an education. Migrant or transient students usually have an interrupted education due to frequent family moves for seasonal employment, and thus these students may be academically behind.

Program	Program Definition
Bilingual / Dual Language	A Bilingual Program is one that helps students who do not speak, read, or write English to become proficient in it. Dual Language Programs (DLPs) are a part of bilingual education, but they are specifically designed to help students become proficient in more than one language (e.g., Spanish and English). There are many types of DLPs, but the most common is a two-way DLP, in which two languages are taught throughout a school year. For instance, DLPs can be designed to meet the needs of the student population found within a school district. Some DLPs are divided into percentages spent on English and another language (e.g., 50/50, 60/40, 80/20). Two-way DLPs have an ESL teacher teaching English and a bilingual teacher teaching the other language. These teachers share the same students throughout a school year. Another type of DLP is a one-way program. In this type of program, one teacher usually teaches both English and another language in the same classroom, with the same students all year long.

Who Qualifies	What Campus Leaders Must Know
Usually a school district will offer a bilingual program only if there are 15–20 students who speak the same foreign language. If there are not enough students to create one class, those students receive services through an ESL or ELL program. In DLP programs, students who speak the foreign language are automatically placed in the DLP classroom. Those students who speak only English usually go through a screening process that predicts which of them will be able to sustain the arduous dual curriculum. This screening process may include a kindergarten aptitude test, a family interview, and a motor skills activity.	Many bilingual and dual language programs start at the kindergarten level and end at the sixth grade level. The premise for bilingual and DLP programs is that it takes about six years for a student to become proficient in reading, writing, and speaking a language. After these six years, or by the time a student reaches the middle grades, a student who is still not proficient in English will attend ESL or ELL classes. A student whose English is proficient by this time may then pursue learning another foreign language. Some schools and school districts have a contract that both students and parents must sign and abide by. This contract may state that the student must stay in the DLP until completion of the sixth grade or upon "graduation" from the program and that the parents must attend all DLP teacher-parent conferences and meetings.

Program	Program Definition
Talented and Gifted (TAG)	TAG programs cater to those students who are deemed highly intelligent, talented, gifted, and creative. These type of programs are designed to allow students to experience learning that may not be traditional but may be more expressive. A TAG program can be held in a self-contained classroom, called a cluster, or as a pull-out program.
Response to Intervention (RtI)	RtI is a relatively new special program. It was established through the reauthorization of the Individuals with Disabilities Education Act in 2004, as an early intervention program. Many schools and school districts are in the process of implementing an RtI program, because it is a regular education program for all students. The purpose of RtI is to find the necessary academic and behavioral interventions and strategies to help students succeed in the regular education classroom, through the regular education teacher.

Who Qualifies	What Campus Leaders Must Know
Students usually qualify for TAG by taking a series of assessments, like an intelligence quotient (IQ) test and a creativity survey/assessment. Some schools may also have students collect teacher recommendations and go through an interview process.	Sometimes students who seem bored or lazy may be perfect candidates for TAG. These types of students may be waiting for a challenge for their intelligence or an outlet for their creativity.
Students who are struggling academically or behaviorally may be referred to the RtI team. This team determines which interventions and strategies a student needs in order to succeed in the regular education setting. Using a three- or four-tier process, an RtI team will collect data from the teachers assigned to the student and monitor the student's progress throughout a specified period. At the end of that period, a student who is making sufficient progress will stay at that tier, continuing to use the same interventions and strategies. A student who is not making adequate progress by the end of the period may be moved up to the next tier, which includes more rigorous interventions. If the lower tiers fail to help the student make adequate progress, and the student reaches the top tier, he or she will eventually be recommended for special education testing.	RtI is a regular education special program. It is not a part of special education. RtI is an early intervention program that is designed to keep more students in regular education classrooms and not refer them too quickly for special education services. It is also designed to help correctly identify students who need special education services. The main tenets of RtI are • Early intervention • Positive behavior instruction • Data-driven decisions • Rigorous and intense interventions • Monitoring

Program	Program Definition
Special Education	Special education is a program grounded by a very powerful federal law, the Individuals with Disabilities Education Act (IDEA). This is one of the most common special programs and is found on most campuses.

Who Qualifies	What Campus Leaders Must Know
In most cases, students must go through the RtI process before being recommended for special education testing. The testing encompasses a plethora of data, including teacher observations, a home survey, a language survey, a medical survey, an achievement assessment, a cognitive assessment, and a behavioral survey and assessment. Once these data are collected, a committee of educators, the parents, and the student is convened to discuss qualification and placement. In rarer cases, a student who has been identified for special education services before age four through Child Find will already have an Individualized Family Service Plan (IFSP) before enrolling in school. The IFSP is usually replaced or supplemented with an Individualized Education Program (IEP) when the student enters pre-kindergarten, a Preschool Program for Children with Disabilities (PPCD), or kindergarten. Hence, a student with an IFSP has already been identified as qualifying for special education services and does not need to go through the RtI process. A child must have an educational need along with a disability in order to qualify for special education services. The qualifying disabilities are: • Autism spectrum disorder (AU or ASD) • Visually impaired (VI) • Auditory impaired (AI)	Various kinds of special education classrooms found on campuses may have been given a special name by a school or school district, such as Life Skills, Severe and Profound, Behavior Management, Vocational Adjustment, Resource, and Content Mastery. In special education, modifications and an IEP are key. Modifications are techniques, strategies, tools, or types of instruction that are provided to help a student succeed in the regular education classroom. An IEP is written for the individual student and outlines the goals and objectives for that student during a determined school year. Prepare yourself ahead of time for an IEP or ARD (Admission, Review, and Dismissal) meeting within your school district by seeking to understand the expectations of the meeting. Signing any IEP/ARD documents in a meeting binds you to follow through with what is outlined in the paperwork. If you have questions, ask them immediately, and ask for training as necessary.

(Continued)

Program	Program Definition
Special Education *(Continued)*	
Section 504	Section 504, or simply "504," is a regular education special program. It is a federally mandated program to help students who need accommodations in school in order to succeed academically and behaviorally.

Who Qualifies	What Campus Leaders Must Know
• Intellectually disabled (ID) or mentally retarded (MR) • Learning disabled (LD) • Traumatic brain injury (TBI) • Other health impaired (OHI) • Emotionally disabled (ED) • Speech or language impairment (SI) • Orthopedic impairment (OI)	
Students who qualify for 504 must have a disability or impairment that substantially limits a life activity. For children, a life activity would be learning in school.	Many schools have an over-representation of students in their 504 program. However, students should be placed in 504 programs only when there is medical proof of a disability or impairment for a long period of time. Many students who are diagnosed as having ADD (attention deficit disorder) or ADHD (attention deficit hyperactivity disorder) are sometimes classified as 504 students. Some students who have cancer or a prosthetic may also be classified as 504 students.

2. The Student Must Show an Interest, Meet a Grade-Level or Other Determinant, or Qualify for Services by Meeting Certain Requirements

Program	Program Definition
Career and Technology Education (CATE)	CATE is a program that focuses on career choices students may make, providing technology education to help students gain marketable skills as job seekers. CATE programs vary from school to school, and from district to district, but many of the same kinds of classes are offered. The following are examples of courses that a CATE program may offer. • Agricultural science and technology • Family and consumer sciences • Health science technology • Business and marketing • Technology • Robotics • Criminal justice • Hospitality and culinary arts • Auto mechanics and auto body repair • Engineering sciences
Early College and Dual Credit	Early College and Dual Credit programs are offered in some high schools to help students attend college and successfully complete college courses. Students are able to earn college credit toward an associate degree or a bachelor's degree, and in some cases, students may complete an associate degree upon graduation from high school. Both Early College and Dual Credit programs are shared between high schools and a community college or *(Continued)*

Who Qualifies	What Campus Leaders Must Know
Most students qualify by being in a certain grade level. Many CATE programs start in middle school with classes that focus on keyboarding, computers and technology, or family and consumer sciences. CATE classes that focus on certification and skilled proficiency, like cosmetology and auto mechanics, are not offered until the junior or senior grade level.	CATE is an excellent avenue for many students, because it exposes them to possible career choices. These are arduous courses and should not be used as a dumping ground for students who "just need to take something" to fill their schedule. Many CATE classrooms at the high school level are in a specialized building off campus.
High school juniors and seniors who have the required and recommended credits may participate in Early College and Dual Credit programs. In some cases, an application, an essay, and teacher recommendations are needed for a student to qualify.	Some school districts pay the college/ university tuition for students through a contract with the local college/ university. Students who participate in this program are usually on the high school campus part of the day and at the college or university the rest of the day. Transportation to and from campuses may be provided by the school district or may be the student's responsibility.

Program	Program Definition
Early College and Dual Credit *(Continued)*	university. In their junior and senior years, students can take courses at the community college or university, earning college freshman and sophomore credit toward a degree that also counts as junior- and senior-level high school credit.
Advanced Placement (AP), International Baccalaureate (IB), Humanities	AP courses are college-level courses taken during the high school years to earn college credit, after students pass an exam given by the College Board. IB courses are part of a specially designed curriculum vetted by the International Baccalaureate Organization. IB schools can be found at the elementary, middle/junior high, and high school levels. The rigor of the curriculum prepares students to continue their studies at military academies, Ivy League universities, and international universities. Humanities courses are found at the high school level. They usually combine an English class with a social studies class, taught by a teacher who is certified in TAG. These courses encourage creativity and expression while also covering the English and social studies curriculum.
Advancement Via Individual Determination (AVID)	AVID is a college-preparatory program for students who may be the first member of their family to attend college.

Who Qualifies	What Campus Leaders Must Know
To qualify for any of these programs, students must show aptitude in understanding, completing, and succeeding in courses with very high expectations and much coursework.

These programs are rigorous, so many schools have an application process that includes an interview, a written essay, and recommendations from teachers. | AP courses are usually taught on a high school campus, and the College Board exams are taken there as well. Pre-AP courses are prep courses usually offered at middle/junior high campuses. A student who excels in a Pre-AP course can take the AP course the following year.

An IB school goes through a rigorous application, monitoring, and evaluation process annually. Teachers at an IB school must go through special training.

Humanities classrooms use the TAG curriculum, so TAG policies and procedures apply to this program. |
| Students who have been designated as "bubble" or "on the cusp" students may qualify for AVID. This program can be implemented at the elementary, middle/junior high, and high school levels, and many universities and colleges are also implementing AVID to help students. | AVID programs are pull-out programs but also can be a specified class on a student's schedule.

This program helps students learn smarter by studying smarter, using tools like Cornell notes, the Socratic method, and peer tutoring to build academic confidence. In AVID classrooms, teachers facilitate learning rather than teaching directly. |

Program	Program Definition
Alternative Education Placement (AEP)	There are several types of alternative education placements or centers. The first is an Academic Alternative Education Placement (AAEP), also referred to as a school with a particular academic specialty. Some school districts call these charter, academy, or magnet schools—for example, the Fine Arts Magnet Academy, the Science and Math Academy, and the Leadership Charter.
	The second type of AEP provides nontraditional settings for learning. This type of AEP caters to students who are nontraditional learners or who do not succeed in a traditional educational setting. A nontraditional AEP might be a school for pregnant students, for example, or a school that helps students who do not have enough credits to graduate from high school and are too old to attend a regular high school.
	The third type of AEP is a Discipline Alternative Education Placement (DAEP). Students who go through a hearing process after committing multiple violations of the Student Code of Conduct are placed in a DAEP.

Who Qualifies	What Campus Leaders Must Know
Students seeking to attend an AAEP usually have to apply. An interview, a written essay, and aptitude test scores may also be required. Students are usually referred by counselors to attend a nontraditional AEP, or they may apply to the school after they are a certain age (e.g., 17 years old). The main point of this type of AEP is to keep students from dropping out by helping them earn a high school diploma in a nontraditional classroom setting. A DAEP is usually found on a separate campus, but some elementary DAEPs are designated classrooms on certain regular campuses.	An AAEP can be a school within a school, with the two schools sharing the same campus but housed in different buildings or different parts of the same building. Some AAEPs are housed on a separate campus. An AEP can be set up in a number of ways and is usually housed on a campus by itself. To accommodate students' work and family schedules, an AEP may be open from 7 a.m. to 7 p.m. on weekdays and also have weekend hours. AEPs may also have computer-based curriculum courses that are self-paced. A student placed at a DAEP must stay for a specified amount of time. The hearing officer at the student's disciplinary hearing will let the committee know how many days a student must attend the DAEP and whether good behavior will lessen the stay. Some state codes specify at what age a student may be sent to a DAEP. For students who are not at an arrestable age (e.g., nine and under), elementary campuses must provide designated classrooms that provide counseling, behavior modification lessons, and rehabilitative services. These students may still participate in campus activities, like lunch, assemblies, and recess, but through the DAEP classroom. For elementray, middle, and high school students of arrestable ages, a separate DAEP campus is provided, with similar services but more restrictions, like expecting students to wear uniforms,. go through metal detectors daily, and work in individual cubicles.

3. The School or School District Must Qualify for Governmental Funds

Program	Program Definition
Title I	Title I is a federally funded program at the elementary, middle/junior high, and high school levels. It provides funding to schools with a high percentage of students who are classified as economically disadvantaged. The purpose of Title I is to even the playing field, providing necessary academic tools to students as they meet the rigorous state and local curriculum requirements.
TRIO Higher Education Programs	The TRIO Programs are federal programs designed to assist students from disadvantaged backgrounds through grants to educational institutions. Some TRIO programs help students find financial aid or educational grants.
Pilot Programs	In some states, pilot programs are implemented before a full-blown program is funded.

Who Qualifies	What Campus Leaders Must Know
A school campus submits data regarding the economic situation of its students' families to the state educational agency. A campus will qualify for funds according to a formula for calculating the proportion of economically disadvantaged students in the student body.	Usually through a plan of action called a Campus Improvement Plan, a Title I campus must designate how its students will be educated and what methods will be used to encourage academic success, such as Saturday school or parent nights. The best way to help the students achieve their potential is to provide an excellent and equal education— one that is differentiated and individualized for each student.
TRIO consists of eight programs for students who may be first-generation college students, who are disabled, or who are low-income.	TRIO programs are offered on high school and college/university campuses. The most common TRIO programs are • Upward Bound • Talent Search • Student Support Services
School districts and schools qualify by either volunteering or being selected to participate based on specific data and variables (e.g., demographics of the students or teachers). Action research is conducted at these districts and campuses to gather the required data.	The purpose of pilot programs is to help a state, school district, or school assess the merits of a given instructional strategy, such as online classes versus face-to-face classes, and decide whether it should become a mandate throughout the school system. A pilot program can be monitored, evaluated, and tweaked before the full program is implemented on a grander scale.

APPENDIX B

Health- and Food-Related Excerpts from the Statutory Codes of the US Government and Selected States

US Code of Regulations (Link)

Title 7—Agriculture
Part 210: National School Lunch Program

This portion of the US Code of Regulations covers the Department of Agriculture's administration of federal child nutrition programs and their requirements for educators. For the full text of this portion of code, see the document at www.fns.usda.gov/cnd/Governance/regulations/7cfr210_12.pdf.

Alabama Education Code (Excerpt)

Section 16-30-4: Presentation of Certificate upon Initial Entrance into School
The boards of education and the governing authority of each private school shall require each pupil who is otherwise entitled to admittance to kindergarten or first grade, whichever is applicable, or any other entrance into an Alabama public or private school, to present a certification of immunization or testing for the prevention of those communicable diseases designated by the State Health Officer, except as provided in Section 16-30-3. Provided, however, that any student presently enrolled in a school in this state, not having been immunized upon initial entrance to school, is hereby required to present a certification of immunization as described in this section upon commencement of the next school year. Section 16-30-1 and this section shall apply only to kindergarten through 12th grade and not to the institutions of higher learning.

(Acts 1973, No. 1269, p. 2113, §4; Acts 1979, No. 79-677, p. 1208, §2.)

Florida K-20 Education Code (Excerpt)

1006.062 Administration of medication and provision of medical services by district school board personnel.

(1) Notwithstanding the provisions of the Nurse Practice Act, part I of chapter 464, district school board personnel may assist students in the administration of prescription medication when the following conditions have been met:

(a) Each district school board shall include in its approved school health services plan a procedure to provide training, by a registered nurse, a licensed practical nurse, a physician licensed pursuant to chapter 458 or chapter 459, or a physician assistant licensed pursuant to chapter 458 or chapter 459, to the school personnel designated by the school principal to assist students in the administration of prescribed medication. Such training may be provided in collaboration with other school districts, through contract with an education consortium, or by any other arrangement consistent with the intent of this subsection.

(b) Each district school board shall adopt policies and procedures governing the administration of prescription medication by district school board personnel. The policies and procedures shall include, but not be limited to, the following provisions:

1. For each prescribed medication, the student's parent shall provide to the school principal a written statement which grants to the school principal or the principal's designee permission to assist in the administration of such medication and which explains the necessity for the medication to be provided during the school day, including any occasion when the student is away from school property on official school business. The school principal or the principal's trained designee shall assist the student in the administration of the medication.

2. Each prescribed medication to be administered by district school board personnel shall be received, counted, and stored in its original container. When the medication is not in use, it shall be stored in its original container in a secure fashion under lock and key in a location designated by the school principal.

(2) There shall be no liability for civil damages as a result of the administration of the medication when the person administering the medication acts as an ordinarily reasonably prudent person would have acted under the same or similar circumstances.

(3) Nonmedical district school board personnel shall not be allowed to perform invasive medical services that require special medical knowledge, nursing judgment, and nursing assessment, including, but not limited to:

(a) Sterile catheterization.

(b) Nasogastric tube feeding.

(c) Cleaning and maintaining a tracheostomy and deep suctioning of a tracheostomy.

(4) Nonmedical assistive personnel shall be allowed to perform health-related services upon successful completion of child-specific training by a registered nurse or advanced registered nurse practitioner licensed under chapter 464, a physician licensed pursuant to chapter 458 or chapter 459, or a physician assistant licensed pursuant to chapter 458 or chapter 459. All procedures shall be monitored periodically by a nurse, advanced registered nurse practitioner, physician assistant, or physician, including, but not limited to:

(a) Intermittent clean catheterization.

(b) Gastrostomy tube feeding.

(c) Monitoring blood glucose.

(d) Administering emergency injectable medication.

(5) For all other invasive medical services not listed in this subsection, a registered nurse or advanced registered nurse practitioner licensed under chapter 464, a physician licensed pursuant to chapter 458 or chapter 459, or a physician assistant licensed pursuant to chapter 458 or chapter 459 shall determine if nonmedical district school board personnel shall be allowed to perform such service.

(6) Each district school board shall establish emergency procedures in accordance with [1]s. 381.0056(5) for life-threatening emergencies.

(7) District school board personnel shall not refer students to or offer students at school facilities contraceptive services without the consent of a parent or legal guardian. To the extent that this subsection conflicts with any provision of chapter 381, the provisions of chapter 381 control.

History.—s. 274, ch. 2002-387.

[1]Note.—Redesignated as s. 381.0056(4) by s. 27, ch. 2012-184.

Maine Revised Statutes (Excerpts)

Title 20-A: Education
Part 3: Elementary and Secondary Education
Chapter 223: Health, Nutrition and Safety
Subchapter 3: School Health Services

§6403-A. School nurse

Each school board shall appoint at least one school nurse for the school administrative unit. [1985, c. 258, §4 (NEW).]

1. Duties. The school nurse shall supervise and coordinate the health services and health-related activities required by this Title.

[1985, c. 258, §4 (NEW).]

2. Other functions. The school nurse shall also perform such other health-related activities as are assigned by the school board.

[1985, c. 258, §4 (NEW).]

3. Appointment. To fulfill the role of school nurse, the school board shall appoint a registered professional nurse who meets any additional certification requirements established by the state board.

[1985, c. 258, §4 (NEW).]

4. Special contract for services. The school board may provide school nurse services through special agreements with a public health agency. All nurses who serve as school nurses under those agreements shall be registered professional nurses who meet applicable certification requirements.

[1985, c. 258, §4 (NEW).]

5. Guidelines. The commissioner shall issue guidelines on the provision of school health services and health-related activities.

[1985, c. 258, §4 (NEW).]

SECTION HISTORY: 1985, c. 258, §4 (NEW).

Subchapter 7: School Lunch and Milk Program

§6602. School food service programs

Public schools shall provide nonprofit school food service programs as follows. [1981, c. 693, §§5, 8 (NEW).]

1. Participation. A public school shall participate in food service programs.

A. A public school shall participate in the National School Lunch Program in accordance with 7 Code of Federal Regulations, Part 210 (2007) and provide Type A meals as determined by the

United States Department of Agriculture. [2007, c. 539, Pt. IIII, §1 (NEW).]

B. A public school that serves breakfast shall provide all students who are eligible for free and reduced-price meals under paragraph A a meal that meets the requirements of the federal School Breakfast Program set forth in 7 Code of Federal Regulations, Part 220 (2007) at no cost to the student. The State shall provide funding equal to the difference between the federal reimbursement for a free breakfast and the federal reimbursement for a reduced-price breakfast for each student eligible for a reduced-price breakfast and receiving breakfast. [2007, c. 539, Pt. IIII, §1 (NEW).]

C. A school administrative unit may participate in the federal summer food service program for children established in 42 United States Code, Section 1761. The commissioner shall assist school administrative units subject to the requirements of this paragraph in developing a plan to participate in the federal summer food service program for children and in obtaining federal, state and private funds to pay for this program. Beginning with the 2011-2012 school year, a school administrative unit with at least one public school in which the percentage of students who qualify for a free or reduced-price lunch is determined to be equal to or greater than the minimum percentage established for eligibility under the National School Lunch Program described in paragraph A may participate in the federal summer food service program for children in accordance with 42 United States Code, Section 1761, subject to the following phase-in schedule:

(1) For the summer following the 2011-2012 school year, a school administrative unit with at least one public school in which at least 75% of students qualified for a free or reduced-price lunch in the 2011-2012 school year may participate in the federal summer food service program;

(2) For the summer following the 2012-2013 school year, a school administrative unit with at least one public school in which at least 65% of students qualified for a free or reduced-price lunch in the 2012-2013 school year may participate in the federal summer food service program; and

(3) For the summer following the 2013-2014 school year and each subsequent school year, a school administrative unit with at least one public school in which at least 50% of students qualified for a free or reduced-price lunch in that school year may participate in the federal summer food service program. [2011, c. 379, §4 (NEW).]

[2011, c. 379, §4 (AMD).]

2. Exceptions. The following are exempt from subsection 1, paragraphs A and B:

A. All secondary schools limited to students in grades 9, 10, 11 and 12; and [1981, c. 693, §§5, 8 (NEW).]

B. A school administrative unit authorized by the commissioner under subsection 9 to postpone the establishment of the program. [1981, c. 693, §§5, 8 (NEW).]

[2011, c. 379, §5 (AMD).]

3. Administration. The school board shall administer and operate the food service programs. The school board:

A. Shall make all contracts to provide material, personnel and equipment necessary to carry out section 6601; and [1981, c. 693, §§5, 8 (NEW).]

B. Shall hire the necessary employees to manage and operate their school food service programs. [1981, c. 693, §§5, 8 (NEW).]

[1981, c. 693, §§5, 8 (NEW).]

4. Funds. The following shall be used to pay for the administration and operation of food service programs:

A. State funds, gifts and appropriations for school food service programs; and [1981, c. 693, §§5, 8 (NEW).]

B. Receipts from the sale of meals under food service programs. [1981, c. 693, §§5, 8 (NEW).]

[1981, c. 693, §§5, 8 (NEW).]

5. Rules. The commissioner shall adopt or amend, with the state board's approval, rules under this subchapter, including rules about the qualifications of food service programs' personnel and rules to implement the federal summer food service program for children under subsection 1, paragraph C.
[2011, c. 379, §6 (AMD).]

6. Nutrition report. The commissioner may assess the nutritional benefits of school lunch programs and school breakfast programs and report to the state board.
[2007, c. 539, Pt. IIII, §2 (AMD).]

7. Technical assistance. The commissioner may give technical assistance to a school board concerning a food service program and may assist in training food service program personnel.
[1981, c. 693, §§5, 8 (NEW).]

8. Application for postponement. An administrative unit, which had been authorized by the commissioner to postpone the establishment of a National School Lunch Program, may apply to the commissioner for a renewal of the postponement. The commissioner may grant the requested postponement provided that:

A. The school board has held a public hearing on its proposed application; and [1981, c. 693, §§5, 8 (NEW).]

B. One of the following conditions is met:

   (1) It has been documented to the commissioner›s satisfaction that the administrative unit lacks space for the program and there is no appropriate alternative source of meals for the students;

   (2) It is impossible for the administrative unit to contract for or to otherwise procure Type A meals for its students; or

   (3) The lack of need for the program, as determined by the school board is documented to the commissioner›s satisfaction and was evident at the public hearing. [1983, c. 422, §18 (AMD).]

If the postponement is granted for the conditions in paragraph B, subparagraphs (1) and (2), it shall be for 3 years. If the postponement is granted for the condition in paragraph B, subparagraph (3), it shall be for 4 years.

[1987, c. 395, Pt. A, §68 (AMD).]

8-A. State board review of commissioner's decisions. A school administrative unit or interested parties may request that the state board reconsider decisions made by the commissioner in subsection 8. The state board shall have the authority to overturn decisions made by the commissioner. In exercising this power, the state board is limited by this section.
[1987, c. 395, Pt. A, §69 (NEW).]

9. Annual review of postponement. The commissioner shall annually review the conditions in the school administrative units which have been granted a postponement. On finding that the conditions in a unit have changed so that a postponement is no longer warranted, the commissioner may require that the unit establish a National School Lunch Program at the start of the next school year.

[1981, c. 693, §§5, 8 (NEW).]

10. Petition by 1% of residential unit. Whenever petitioned by 1% of the residents of a unit, the commissioner shall call a public hearing on the postponement prior to the next annual review.

[1981, c. 693, §§5, 8 (NEW).]

11. The state may administer. The state may administer the programs under the United States Child Nutrition Act, Public Law 89-642 in nonprofit, private schools, provided that the State shall not be required to appropriate or distribute state funds for meals served in private schools to those private schools.

[1983, c. 276, (NEW).]

12. Local Produce Fund. The Local Produce Fund is established within the Department of Education. The fund is authorized to receive revenue from public and private sources. The fund must be held separate and apart from all other money, funds and accounts. Any balance remaining in the fund at the end of the fiscal year must be carried forward to the next fiscal year. The fund must be used to match $1 for every $3 a school administrative unit pays for produce or minimally processed foods purchased directly from a farmer or farmers' cooperative in the State, to a maximum state contribution of $1,000. At the end of the fiscal year, the school administrative unit may provide the department with receipts documenting purchases pursuant to this subsection during that year. For purposes of this subsection, "minimally processed" means only the washing, cleaning, trimming, drying, sorting and packaging of food items or a combination of those activities. Reimbursement or partial reimbursement to school administrative units may only be made up to the amount available in the fund. Failure to reimburse does not constitute an obligation on behalf of the State to a school administrative unit.

[2001, c. 447, §1 (NEW).]

SECTION HISTORY: 1981, c. 693, §§5,8 (NEW). 1983, c. 276, (AMD). 1983, c. 422, §18 (AMD). 1985, c. 263, (AMD). 1987, c. 395, §§A68,A69 (AMD). 1989, c. 875, §G1 (AMD). 1991, c. 9, §II3 (AMD). 2001, c. 447, §1 (AMD). 2007, c. 539, Pt. IIII, §§1, 2 (AMD). 2011, c. 379, §§4-6 (AMD).

Subchapter 9: Nutrition Education Heading: PL 2005, C. 435, §1 (New)

§6662. Foods outside school meal program

1. Nutritional information. After August 31, 2008, food service programs must post caloric information for prepackaged a la carte menu items at the point-of-decision.

[2005, c. 435, §1 (NEW).]

2. Food and beverages outside school lunch programs. The department shall adopt rules to establish standards for food and beverages sold or distributed on school grounds but outside of school meal programs. These standards must include maximum portion sizes, except for portion sizes for milk, that are consistent with federal school nutrition standards. Rules adopted pursuant to this subsection are major substantive rules as defined in Title 5, chapter 375, subchapter 2-A.

Rules adopted pursuant to this subsection do not apply to food and beverages sold or offered at community events or fund-raisers held outside the hours of the normal school day and to products prepared in culinary arts programs provided by career and technical schools and programs.

[2011, c. 224, §1 (AMD).]

3. Food and beverage advertising. Brand-specific advertising of food or beverages is prohibited in school buildings or on school grounds except for food and beverages meeting standards for sale or distribution on school grounds in accordance with rules adopted under subsection 2.

For the purposes of this subsection, "advertising" does not include advertising on broadcast media or in print media such as newspapers and magazines, clothing with brand images worn on school grounds or advertising on product packaging.

[2007, c. 156, §1 (NEW).]

SECTION HISTORY: 2005, c. 435, §1 (NEW). 2007, c. 156, §1 (AMD). 2011, c. 224, §1 (AMD).

Montana Code Annotated 2011 (Excerpts)

Title 20: Education
Chapter 10: Transportation and Food Services
Part 2: Food Services

20-10-205. Allocation of federal funds to school food services fund for federally connected, indigent pupils. The trustees of any school district receiving federal reimbursement in lieu of taxes may request the allocation of a portion of those federal funds to the school food services fund to provide free meals for federally connected, indigent pupils when the pupils are declared eligible. In granting the request, the county superintendent shall comply with the following procedures:

(1) The indigency must be certified by the local office of public assistance, assisted by a committee of three composed of the county superintendent, a representative of the county health department, and an authorized representative of the district.

(2) A certified, detailed claim for the amount of the federal reimbursement in lieu of taxes that is to be allocated to the school food services fund must be filed by the district with the county superintendent. The county superintendent shall confirm or adjust the amount of the claim by:

(a) determining that the pupils included on the claim have been declared indigent under subsection (1);

(b) determining the number of meals provided the indigent pupils by the school food services;

(c) determining the price for each meal that is charged to the nonindigent pupil; and

(d) multiplying the number of meals provided to indigent pupils by the price for each meal.

(3) After the county superintendent's confirmation or adjustment of the claim, the county superintendent shall notify the district and the county treasurer of the approved amounts for allocation to the school food services fund. The district shall deposit the approved amount in the school food services fund on receipt of the succeeding federal payment in lieu of taxes.

History: En. 75-8006 by Sec. 447, Ch. 5, L. 1971; R.C.M. 1947, 75-8006; amd. Sec. 63, Ch. 114, L. 2003.

Title 50: Health and Safety
Chapter 49: Food and Nutrition
Part 1: Montana Access to Food and Nutrition Act

50-49-102. Purpose. It is the policy of the state of Montana that all citizens should have access to food programs and nutrition services to prevent any needy citizen from experiencing hunger and poor nutrition and their impact on physical and mental health.

History: En. Sec. 1, Ch. 569, L. 1991.

Texas Administrative Code (Link)

Title 4: Agriculture
Part 1: Texas Department of Agriculture
Chapter 26: Food and Nutrition Division
Subchapter A: Texas Public School Nutrition Policy

This portion of the Texas Administrative Code contains the food-related regulations that educators are to follow in public schools. See http://info.sos.state.tx.us/pls/pub/readtac$ext. ViewTAC?tac_view=5&ti=4&pt=1&ch=26&sch=A&rl=Y.

Texas Education Code (Excerpt)

Title 2. Public Education
Subtitle G. Safe Schools
Chapter 38. Health and Safety
Subchapter A. General Provisions

Sec. 38.001. IMMUNIZATION; REQUIREMENTS; EXCEPTIONS. (a) Each student shall be fully immunized against diphtheria, rubeola, rubella, mumps, tetanus, and poliomyelitis, except as provided by Subsection (c).

Text of subsection as amended by Acts 2007, 80th Leg., R.S., Ch. 43, Sec. 1

(b) Subject to Subsections (b-1) and (c), the executive commissioner of the Health and Human Services Commission may modify or delete any of the immunizations in Subsection (a) or may require immunizations against additional diseases as a requirement for admission to any elementary or secondary school.

Text of subsection as amended by Acts 2007, 80th Leg., R.S., Ch. 94, Sec. 2

(b) Subject to Subsection (c), the Department of State Health Services may modify or delete any of the immunizations in Subsection (a) or may require immunizations against additional diseases as a requirement for admission to any elementary or secondary school.

(b-1) Each year, the Department of State Health Services shall prepare a list of the immunizations required under this section for admission to public schools and of any additional immunizations the department recommends for school-age children. The department shall prepare the list in English and Spanish and make the list available in a manner that permits a school district to easily post the list on the district's Internet website as required by Section 38.019.

(c) Immunization is not required for a person's admission to any elementary or secondary school if the person applying for admission:
(1) submits to the admitting official:
(A) an affidavit or a certificate signed by a physician who is duly registered and licensed to practice medicine in the United States, in which it is stated that, in the physician's opinion, the immunization required poses a significant risk to the health and well-being of the applicant or any member of the applicant's family or household; or
(B) an affidavit signed by the applicant or, if a minor, by the applicant's parent or guardian stating that the applicant declines immunization for reasons of conscience, including a religious belief; or
(2) is a member of the armed forces of the United States and is on active duty.

(c-1) An affidavit submitted under Section (c)(1)(B) must be on a form described by Section 161.0041, Health and Safety Code, and must be submitted to the admitting official not later than the 90th day after the date the affidavit is notarized.

(d) The Department of State Health Services shall provide the required immunization to children in areas where no local provision exists to provide those services.

(e) A person may be provisionally admitted to an elementary or secondary school if the person has begun the required immunizations and if the person continues to receive the necessary immunizations as rapidly as is medically feasible. The Department of State Health Services shall adopt rules relating to the provisional admission of persons to an elementary or secondary school.

(f) A person who has not received the immunizations required by this section for reasons of conscience, including because of the person's religious beliefs, may be excluded from school in times of emergency or epidemic declared by the commissioner of public health.

Added by Acts 1995, 74th Leg., ch. 260, Sec. 1, eff. May 30, 1995. Amended by Acts 2003, 78th Leg., ch. 198, Sec. 2.160, eff. Sept. 1, 2003.
Amended by:
 Acts 2007, 80th Leg., R.S., Ch. 43, Sec. 1, eff. May 8, 2007.
 Acts 2007, 80th Leg., R.S., Ch. 94, Sec. 2, eff. May 15, 2007.

Sec. 38.002. IMMUNIZATION RECORDS; REPORTING. (a) Each public school shall keep an individual immunization record during the period of attendance for each student admitted. The records shall be open for inspection at all reasonable times by the Texas Education Agency or by representatives of local health departments or the Texas Department of Health.

(b) Each public school shall cooperate in transferring students' immunization records to other schools. Specific approval from students, parents, or guardians is not required before transferring those records.

(c) The Texas Education Agency and the Texas Department of Health shall develop the form for a required annual report of the immunization status of students. The report shall be submitted by all schools at the time and in the manner indicated in the instructions printed on the form.

Added by Acts 1995, 74th Leg., ch. 260, Sec. 1, eff. May 30, 1995.

Sec. 38.0025. DISSEMINATION OF BACTERIAL MENINGITIS INFORMATION. (a) The agency shall prescribe procedures by which each school district shall provide information relating to bacterial meningitis to its students and their parents each school year. The procedures must ensure that the information is reasonably likely to come to the attention of the parents of each student. The agency shall prescribe the form and content of the information. The information must cover:

(1) the symptoms of the disease, how it may be diagnosed, and its possible consequences if untreated;

(2) how the disease is transmitted, how it may be prevented, and the relative risk of contracting the disease for primary and secondary school students;

(3) the availability and effectiveness of vaccination against and treatment for the disease, and a brief description of the risks and possible side effects of vaccination; and

(4) sources of additional information regarding the disease, including any appropriate office of the school district and the appropriate office of the Texas Department of Health.

(b) The agency shall consult with the Texas Department of Health in prescribing the content of the information to be provided to students under this section. The agency shall establish an advisory committee to assist the agency in the initial implementation of this section. The advisory committee must include at least two members who are parents of students at public schools in this state.

(c) A school district, with the written consent of the agency, may provide the information required by this section to its students and their parents by a method different from the method prescribed by the agency under Subsection (a) if the agency determines that method would be effective in bringing the information to the attention of the parents of each student.

Added by Acts 2001, 77th Leg., ch. 219, Sec. 2, eff. May 22, 2001.

Sec. 38.003. SCREENING AND TREATMENT FOR DYSLEXIA AND RELATED DIS-ORDERS. (a) Students enrolling in public schools in this state shall be tested for dyslexia and related disorders at appropriate times in accordance with a program approved by the State Board of Education.

(b) In accordance with the program approved by the State Board of Education, the board of trustees of each school district shall provide for the treatment of any student determined to have dyslexia or a related disorder.

(b-1) Unless otherwise provided by law, a student determined to have dyslexia during testing under Subsection (a) or accommodated because of dyslexia may not be retested for dyslexia for the purpose of reassessing the student's need for accommodations until the district reevaluates the information obtained from previous testing of the student.

(c) The State Board of Education shall adopt any rules and standards necessary to administer this section.

(d) In this section:

(1) "Dyslexia" means a disorder of constitutional origin manifested by a difficulty in learning to read, write, or spell, despite conventional instruction, adequate intelligence, and sociocultural opportunity.

(2) "Related disorders" includes disorders similar to or related to dyslexia, such as developmental auditory imperception, dysphasia, specific developmental dyslexia, developmental dysgraphia, and developmental spelling disability.

Added by Acts 1995, 74th Leg., ch. 260, Sec. 1, eff. May 30, 1995.
Amended by:
Acts 2011, 82nd Leg., R.S., Ch. 635, Sec. 3, eff. June 17, 2011.

Sec. 38.0031. CLASSROOM TECHNOLOGY PLAN FOR STUDENTS WITH DYSLEX-IA. (a) The agency shall establish a committee to develop a plan for integrating technology into the classroom to help accommodate students with dyslexia. The plan must:

(1) determine the classroom technologies that are useful and practical in assisting public schools in accommodating students with dyslexia, considering budget constraints of school districts; and

(2) develop a strategy for providing those effective technologies to students.

(b) The agency shall provide the plan and information about the availability and benefits of the technologies identified under Subsection (a)(1) to school districts.

(c) A member of the committee established under Subsection (a) is not entitled to reimbursement for travel expenses incurred by the member under this section unless agency funds are available for that purpose.

Added by Acts 2011, 82nd Leg., R.S., Ch. 635, Sec. 4, eff. June 17, 2011.

Sec. 38.004. CHILD ABUSE REPORTING AND PROGRAMS. (a) The agency shall develop a policy governing the child abuse reports required by Chapter 261, Family Code, of school districts and their employees. The policy must provide for cooperation with law enforcement child abuse investigations without the consent of the child's parents if necessary, including investigations by the Department of Protective and Regulatory Services. Each school district shall adopt the policy.

(a-1) The agency shall:

(1) maintain on the agency Internet website a list of links to websites that provide information regarding the prevention of child abuse; and

(2) develop and periodically update a training program on prevention of child abuse that a school district may use for staff development.

(b) Each school district shall provide child abuse antivictimization programs in elementary and secondary schools.

Added by Acts 1995, 74th Leg., ch. 260, Sec. 1, eff. May 30, 1995.

Amended by:
Acts 2007, 80th Leg., R.S., Ch. 561, Sec. 1, eff. June 16, 2007.

Sec. 38.0041. POLICIES ADDRESSING SEXUAL ABUSE AND OTHER MALTREAT-MENT OF CHILDREN. (a) Each school district and open-enrollment charter school shall adopt and implement a policy addressing sexual abuse and other maltreatment of children, to be included in the district improvement plan under Section 11.252 and any informational handbook provided to students and parents.

(b) A policy required by this section must address:

(1) methods for increasing staff, student, and parent awareness of issues regarding sexual abuse and other maltreatment of children, including prevention techniques and knowledge of likely warning signs indicating that a child may be a victim of sexual abuse or other maltreatment, using resources developed by the agency under Section 38.004;

(2) actions that a child who is a victim of sexual abuse or other maltreatment should take to obtain assistance and intervention; and

(3) available counseling options for students affected by sexual abuse or other maltreatment.

(c) The methods under Subsection (b)(1) for increasing awareness of issues regarding sexual abuse and other maltreatment of children must include training, as provided by this subsection, concerning prevention techniques for and recognition of sexual abuse and all other maltreatment of children. The training:

(1) must be provided, as part of a new employee orientation, to new school district and open-enrollment charter school educators, including counselors and coaches, and other district and charter school professional staff members;

(2) may be provided annually to any district or charter school staff member; and

(3) must include training concerning:

(A) factors indicating a child is at risk for sexual abuse or other maltreatment;

(B) likely warning signs indicating a child may be a victim of sexual abuse or other maltreatment;

(C) internal procedures for seeking assistance for a child who is at risk for sexual abuse or other maltreatment, including referral to a school counselor, a social worker, or another mental health professional;

(D) techniques for reducing a child's risk of sexual abuse or other maltreatment; and

(E) community organizations that have relevant existing research-based programs that are able to provide training or other education for school district or open-enrollment charter school staff members, students, and parents.

(d) For any training under Subsection (c), each school district and open-enrollment charter school shall maintain records that include the name of each district or charter school staff member who participated in the training.

(e) If a school district or open-enrollment charter school determines that the district or charter school does not have sufficient resources to provide the training required under Subsection (c), the district or charter school shall work in conjunction with a community organization to provide the training at no cost to the district or charter school.

(f) The training under Subsection (c) may be included in staff development under Section 21.451.

(g) A school district or open-enrollment charter school employee may not be subject to any disciplinary proceeding, as defined by Section 22.0512(b), resulting from an action taken in compliance with this section. The requirements of this section are considered to involve an employee's judgment and discretion and are not considered ministerial acts for purposes of immunity from liability under Section 22.0511. Nothing in this section may be considered to limit the immunity from liability provided under Section 22.0511.

(h) For purposes of this section, "other maltreatment" has the meaning assigned by Section 42.002, Human Resources Code.

Added by Acts 2009, 81st Leg., R.S., Ch. 1115, Sec. 2, eff. June 19, 2009.
Amended by:
Acts 2011, 82nd Leg., R.S., Ch. 1323, Sec. 2, eff. June 17, 2011.

Sec. 38.005. PROTECTIVE EYE DEVICES IN PUBLIC SCHOOLS. Each teacher and student must wear industrial-quality eye-protective devices in appropriate situations as determined by school district policy.

Added by Acts 1995, 74th Leg., ch. 260, Sec. 1, eff. May 30, 1995.

Sec. 38.006. TOBACCO ON SCHOOL PROPERTY. The board of trustees of a school district shall:

(1) prohibit smoking or using tobacco products at a school-related or school-sanctioned activity on or off school property;

(2) prohibit students from possessing tobacco products at a school-related or school-sanctioned activity on or off school property; and

(3) ensure that school personnel enforce the policies on school property.

Added by Acts 1995, 74th Leg., ch. 260, Sec. 1, eff. May 30, 1995.

Sec. 38.007. ALCOHOL-FREE SCHOOL ZONES. (a) The board of trustees of a school district shall prohibit the use of alcoholic beverages at a school-related or school-sanctioned activity on or off school property.

(b) The board of trustees of a school district shall attempt to provide a safe alcohol-free environment to students coming to or going from school. The board of trustees may cooperate with local law enforcement officials and the Texas Alcoholic Beverage Commission in attempting to provide this environment and in enforcing Sections 101.75, 109.33, and 109.59, Alcoholic Beverage Code. Additionally, the board, if a majority of the area of a district is located in a municipality with a population of 900,000 or more, may petition the commissioners court of the county in which the district is located or the governing board of an incorporated city or town in which the district is located to adopt a 1,000-foot zone under Section 109.33, Alcoholic Beverage Code.

Added by Acts 1995, 74th Leg., ch. 260, Sec. 1, eff. May 30, 1995.

Sec. 38.008. POSTING OF STEROID LAW NOTICE. Each school in a school district in which there is a grade level of seven or higher shall post in a conspicuous location in the school gymnasium and each other place in a building where physical education classes are conducted the following notice:

> Anabolic steroids are for medical use only. State law prohibits possessing, dispensing, delivering, or administering an anabolic steroid in any manner not allowed by state law. State law provides that body building, muscle enhancement, or the increase of muscle bulk or strength through the use of an anabolic steroid or human growth hormone by a person who is in good health is not a valid medical purpose. Only a medical doctor may prescribe an anabolic steroid or human growth hormone for a person. A violation of state law concerning anabolic steroids or human growth hormones is a criminal offense punishable by confinement in jail or imprisonment in the Texas Department of Criminal Justice.

Added by Acts 1995, 74th Leg., ch. 260, Sec. 1, eff. May 30, 1995.
Amended by:
Acts 2009, 81st Leg., R.S., Ch. 87, Sec. 25.050, eff. September 1, 2009.

Sec. 38.0081. INFORMATION ABOUT STEROIDS. (a) The agency, in conjunction with the Department of State Health Services, shall:

(1) develop information about the use of anabolic steroids and the health risks involved with such use; and

(2) distribute the information to school districts.

(b) Each school district shall, at appropriate grade levels as determined by the State Board of Education, provide the information developed under Subsection (a) to district students, particularly to those students involved in extracurricular athletic activities.

Added by Acts 2005, 79th Leg., Ch. 1177, Sec. 2, eff. June 18, 2005.

Sec. 38.009. ACCESS TO MEDICAL RECORDS. (a) A school administrator, nurse, or teacher is entitled to access to a student's medical records maintained by the school district for reasons determined by district policy.

(b) A school administrator, nurse, or teacher who views medical records under this section shall maintain the confidentiality of those medical records.

(c) This section does not authorize a school administrator, nurse, or teacher to require a student to be tested to determine the student's medical condition or status.

Added by Acts 1995, 74th Leg., ch. 260, Sec. 1, eff. May 30, 1995.

Sec. 38.0095. PARENTAL ACCESS TO MEDICAL RECORDS. (a) A parent or guardian of a student is entitled to access to the student's medical records maintained by a school district.

(b) On request of a student's parent or guardian, the school district shall provide a copy of the student's medical records to the parent or guardian. The district may not impose a charge for providing the copy that exceeds the charge authorized by Section 552.261, Government Code, for providing a copy of public information.

Added by Acts 1999, 76th Leg., ch. 1418, Sec. 3, eff. June 19, 1999.

Sec. 38.010. OUTSIDE COUNSELORS. (a) A school district or school district employee may not refer a student to an outside counselor for care or treatment of a chemical dependency or an emotional or psychological condition unless the district:

(1) obtains prior written consent for the referral from the student's parent;

(2) discloses to the student's parent any relationship between the district and the outside counselor;

(3) informs the student and the student's parent of any alternative public or private source of care or treatment reasonably available in the area;

(4) requires the approval of appropriate school district personnel before a student may be referred for care or treatment or before a referral is suggested as being warranted; and

(5) specifically prohibits any disclosure of a student record that violates state or federal law.

(b) In this section, "parent" includes a managing conservator or guardian.

Added by Acts 1995, 74th Leg., ch. 260, Sec. 1, eff. May 30, 1995.

Sec. 38.011. DIETARY SUPPLEMENTS. (a) A school district employee may not:

(1) knowingly sell, market, or distribute a dietary supplement that contains performance enhancing compounds to a primary or secondary education student with whom the employee has contact as part of the employee's school district duties; or

(2) knowingly endorse or suggest the ingestion, intranasal application, or inhalation of a dietary supplement that contains performance enhancing compounds by a primary or secondary education student with whom the employee has contact as part of the employee's school district duties.

(b) This section does not prohibit a school district employee from:

(1) providing or endorsing a dietary supplement that contains performance enhancing compounds to, or suggesting the ingestion, intranasal application, or inhalation of a dietary supplement that contains performance enhancing compounds by, the employee's child; or

(2) selling, marketing, or distributing a dietary supplement that contains performance enhancing compounds to, or endorsing or suggesting the ingestion, intranasal application, or inhalation of a dietary supplement that contains performance enhancing compounds by, a primary or secondary education student as part of activities that:

(A) do not occur on school property or at a school-related function;

(B) are entirely separate from any aspect of the employee's employment with the school district; and

(C) do not in any way involve information about or contacts with students that the employee has had access to, directly or indirectly, through any aspect of the employee's employment with the school district.

(c) A person who violates this section commits an offense. An offense under this section is a Class C misdemeanor.

(d) In this section:

(1) "Dietary supplement" has the meaning assigned by 21 U.S.C. Section 321 and its subsequent amendments.

(2) "Performance enhancing compound" means a manufactured product for oral ingestion, intranasal application, or inhalation that:

(A) contains a stimulant, amino acid, hormone precursor, herb or other botanical, or any other substance other than an essential vitamin or mineral; and

(B) is intended to increase athletic or intellectual performance, promote muscle growth, or increase an individual's endurance or capacity for exercise.

Added by Acts 1999, 76th Leg., ch. 1086, Sec. 1, eff. Sept. 1, 1999.

Sec. 38.012. NOTICE CONCERNING HEALTH CARE SERVICES. (a) Before a school district or school may expand or change the health care services available at a school in the district from those that were available on January 1, 1999, the board of trustees must:

(1) hold a public hearing at which the board discloses all information on the proposed health care services, including:

(A) all health care services to be provided;

(B) whether federal law permits or requires any health care service provided to be kept confidential from parents;

(C) whether a child's medical records will be accessible to the child's parent;

(D) information concerning grant funds to be used;

(E) the titles of persons who will have access to the medical records of a student; and

(F) the security measures that will be used to protect the privacy of students' medical records; and

(2) approve the expansion or change by a record vote.

(b) A hearing under Subsection (a) must include an opportunity for public comment on the proposal.

Added by Acts 1999, 76th Leg., ch. 1418, Sec. 2, eff. June 19, 1999.

Sec. 38.013. COORDINATED HEALTH PROGRAM FOR ELEMENTARY, MIDDLE, AND JUNIOR HIGH SCHOOL STUDENTS. (a) The agency shall make available to each school district one or more coordinated health programs designed to prevent obesity, cardiovascular disease, and Type 2 diabetes in elementary school, middle school, and junior high school students. Each program must provide for coordinating:

(1) health education;

(2) physical education and physical activity;

(3) nutrition services; and

(4) parental involvement.

(a-1) The commissioner by rule shall adopt criteria for evaluating a coordinated health program before making the program available under Subsection (a). Before adopting the criteria, the commissioner shall request review and comment concerning the criteria from the Department of State Health Services School Health Advisory Committee. The commissioner may make available under Subsection (a) only those programs that meet criteria adopted under this subsection.

(b) The agency shall notify each school district of the availability of the programs.

(c) The commissioner by rule shall adopt criteria for evaluating the nutritional services component of a program under this section that includes an evaluation of program compliance with the Department of Agriculture guidelines relating to foods of minimal nutritional value.

Added by Acts 2001, 77th Leg., ch. 907, Sec. 3, eff. June 14, 2001. Amended by Acts 2003, 78th Leg., ch. 944, Sec. 3, eff. Sept. 1, 2003.
Amended by:
Acts 2005, 79th Leg., Ch. 784, Sec. 3, eff. June 17, 2005.
Acts 2005, 79th Leg., Ch. 784, Sec. 4, eff. June 17, 2005.

Sec. 38.014. IMPLEMENTATION OF COORDINATED HEALTH PROGRAM FOR ELEMENTARY, MIDDLE, AND JUNIOR HIGH SCHOOL STUDENTS. (a) Each school district shall:

(1) participate in appropriate training for the implementation of the program approved by the agency under Section 38.013; and

(2) implement the program in each elementary school, middle school, and junior high school in the district.

(b) The agency, in cooperation with the Texas Department of Health, shall adopt a schedule for regional education service centers to provide necessary training under this section.

Added by Acts 2001, 77th Leg., ch. 907, Sec. 3, eff. June 14, 2001.
Amended by:
Acts 2005, 79th Leg., Ch. 784, Sec. 5, eff. June 17, 2005.
Acts 2005, 79th Leg., Ch. 784, Sec. 6, eff. June 17, 2005.

Sec. 38.0141. REPORTING OF CERTAIN HEALTH AND SAFETY INFORMATION REQUIRED. Each school district shall provide to the agency information as required by the commissioner, including statistics and data, relating to student health and physical activity and information described by Section 28.004(k), presented in a form determined by the commissioner. The district shall provide the information required by this section for the district and for each campus in the district.

Added by Acts 2005, 79th Leg., Ch. 784, Sec. 7, eff. June 17, 2005.

Sec. 38.015. SELF-ADMINISTRATION OF PRESCRIPTION ASTHMA OR ANAPHYLAXIS MEDICINE BY STUDENTS. (a) In this section:

(1) "Parent" includes a person standing in parental relation.

(2) "Self-administration of prescription asthma or anaphylaxis medicine" means a student's discretionary use of prescription asthma or anaphylaxis medicine.

(b) A student with asthma or anaphylaxis is entitled to possess and self-administer prescription asthma or anaphylaxis medicine while on school property or at a school-related event or activity if:

(1) the prescription medicine has been prescribed for that student as indicated by the prescription label on the medicine;

(2) the student has demonstrated to the student's physician or other licensed health care provider and the school nurse, if available, the skill level necessary to self-administer the prescription medication, including the use of any device required to administer the medication;

(3) the self-administration is done in compliance with the prescription or written instructions from the student's physician or other licensed health care provider; and

(4) a parent of the student provides to the school:

(A) a written authorization, signed by the parent, for the student to self-administer the prescription medicine while on school property or at a school-related event or activity; and

(B) a written statement from the student's physician or other licensed health care provider, signed by the physician or provider, that states:

(i) that the student has asthma or anaphylaxis and is capable of self-administering the prescription medicine;

(ii) the name and purpose of the medicine;

(iii) the prescribed dosage for the medicine;

(iv) the times at which or circumstances under which the medicine may be administered; and

(v) the period for which the medicine is prescribed.

(c) The physician's statement must be kept on file in the office of the school nurse of the school the student attends or, if there is not a school nurse, in the office of the principal of the school the student attends.

(d) This section does not:

(1) waive any liability or immunity of a governmental unit or its officers or employees; or

(2) create any liability for or a cause of action against a governmental unit or its officers or employees.

(e) The commissioner may adopt rules and prescribe forms to assist in the implementation of this section.

Added by Acts 2001, 77th Leg., ch. 511, Sec. 1, eff. June 11, 2001. Renumbered from Education Code Sec. 38.013 by Acts 2003, 78th Leg., ch. 1275, Sec. 2(19), eff. Sept. 1, 2003.
Amended by:
Acts 2006, 79th Leg., 3rd C.S., Ch. 5, Sec. 10.01, eff. May 31, 2006.
Acts 2006, 79th Leg., 3rd C.S., Ch. 5, Sec. 10.02, eff. May 31, 2006.

Sec. 38.0151. POLICIES FOR CARE OF CERTAIN STUDENTS AT RISK FOR ANAPHYLAXIS. (a) The board of trustees of each school district and the governing body or an appropriate officer of each open-enrollment charter school shall adopt and administer a policy for the care of students with a diagnosed food allergy at risk for anaphylaxis based on guidelines developed by the commissioner of state health services in consultation with an ad hoc committee appointed by the commissioner of state health services.

(b) A school district or open-enrollment charter school that implemented a policy for the care of students with a diagnosed food allergy at risk for anaphylaxis before the development of the guidelines described by Subsection (a) shall review the policy and revise the policy as necessary to ensure the policy is consistent with the guidelines.

(b-1) Expired.

(b-2) Expired.

(b-3) Expired.

(b-4) Expired.

(c) The guidelines described by Subsection (a) may not:

(1) require a school district or open-enrollment charter school to purchase prescription anaphylaxis medication, such as epinephrine, or require any other expenditure that would result in a negative fiscal impact on the district or charter school; or

(2) require the personnel of a district or charter school to administer anaphylaxis medication, such as epinephrine, to a student unless the anaphylaxis medication is prescribed for that student.

(d) This section does not:

(1) waive any liability or immunity of a governmental entity or its officers or employees; or

(2) create any liability for or a cause of action against a governmental entity or its officers or employees.

(e) The agency shall post the guidelines developed by the commissioner of state health services under this section on the agency's website with any other information relating to students with special health needs.

Added by Acts 2011, 82nd Leg., R.S., Ch. 590, Sec. 1, eff. June 17, 2011.

Sec. 38.016. PSYCHOTROPIC DRUGS AND PSYCHIATRIC EVALUATIONS OR EXAMINATIONS. (a) In this section:

(1) "Parent" includes a guardian or other person standing in parental relation.

(2) "Psychotropic drug" means a substance that is:

(A) used in the diagnosis, treatment, or prevention of a disease or as a component of a medication; and

(B) intended to have an altering effect on perception, emotion, or behavior.

(b) A school district employee may not:

(1) recommend that a student use a psychotropic drug; or

(2) suggest any particular diagnosis; or

(3) use the refusal by a parent to consent to administration of a psychotropic drug to a student or to a psychiatric evaluation or examination of a student as grounds, by itself, for prohibiting the child from attending a class or participating in a school-related activity.

(c) Subsection (b) does not:

(1) prevent an appropriate referral under the child find system required under 20 U.S.C. Section 1412, as amended; or

(2) prohibit a school district employee who is a registered nurse, advanced nurse practitioner, physician, or certified or appropriately credentialed mental health professional from recommending that a child be evaluated by an appropriate medical practitioner; or

(3) prohibit a school employee from discussing any aspect of a child's behavior or academic progress with the child's parent or another school district employee.

(d) The board of trustees of each school district shall adopt a policy to ensure implementation and enforcement of this section.

(e) An act in violation of Subsection (b) does not override the immunity from personal liability granted in Section 22.0511 or other law or the district's sovereign and governmental immunity.

Added by Acts 2003, 78th Leg., ch. 1058, Sec. 1, eff. June 20, 2003.
Amended by:
Acts 2007, 80th Leg., R.S., Ch. 921, Sec. 4.008, eff. September 1, 2007.

Sec. 38.017. AVAILABILITY OF AUTOMATED EXTERNAL DEFIBRILLATOR. (a) Each school district shall make available at each campus in the district at least one automated external defibrillator, as defined by Section 779.001, Health and Safety Code. A campus defibrillator must be readily available during any University Interscholastic League athletic competition held on the campus. In determining the location at which to store a campus defibrillator, the principal of the campus shall consider the primary location on campus where students engage in athletic activities.

(b) To the extent practicable, each school district, in cooperation with the University Interscholastic League, shall make reasonable efforts to ensure that an automated external defibrillator is available at each University Interscholastic League athletic practice held at a district campus. If a school district is not able to make an automated external defibrillator available in the manner provided by this subsection, the district shall determine the extent to which an automated external defibrillator must be available at each University Interscholastic League athletic practice held at a district campus. The determination must be based, in addition to any other appropriate considerations, on relevant medical information.

(c) Each school district, in cooperation with the University Interscholastic League, shall determine the extent to which an automated external defibrillator must be available at each University Interscholastic League athletic competition held at a location other than a district campus. The determination must be based, in addition to any other appropriate considerations, on relevant medical information and whether emergency services personnel are present at the athletic competition under a contract with the school district.

(d) Each school district shall ensure the presence at each location at which an automated external defibrillator is required under Subsection (a), (b), or (c) of at least one campus or district employee trained in the proper use of the defibrillator at any time a substantial number of district students are present at the location.

(e) A school district shall ensure that an automated external defibrillator is used and maintained in accordance with standards established under Chapter 779, Health and Safety Code.

(f) This section does not:

(1) waive any immunity from liability of a school district or its officers or employees;

(2) create any liability for or a cause of action against a school district or its officers or employees; or

(3) waive any immunity from liability under Section 74.151, Civil Practice and Remedies Code.

(g) This subsection applies only to a private school that receives an automated external defibrillator from the agency or receives funding from the agency to purchase or lease an automated external defibrillator. A private school shall:

(1) make available at the school at least one automated external defibrillator; and

(2) in coordination with the Texas Association of Private and Parochial Schools, adopt a policy concerning the availability of an automated external defibrillator at athletic competitions and practices in a manner consistent with the requirements prescribed by this section, including the training and maintenance requirements prescribed by this section.

(h) A school district may seek and accept gifts, grants, or other donations to pay the district's cost of purchasing automated external defibrillators required under this section.

Added by Acts 2007, 80th Leg., R.S., Ch. 1371, Sec. 6, eff. June 15, 2007.

Sec. 38.018. PROCEDURES REGARDING RESPONSE TO CARDIAC ARREST. (a) Each school district and private school shall develop safety procedures for a district or school employee or student to follow in responding to a medical emergency involving cardiac arrest, including the appropriate response time in administering cardiopulmonary resuscitation, using an automated external defibrillator, as defined by Section 779.001, Health and Safety Code, or calling a local emergency medical services provider.

(b) A private school is required to develop safety procedures under this section only if the school receives an automated external defibrillator from the agency or receives funding from the agency to purchase or lease an automated external defibrillator.

Added by Acts 2007, 80th Leg., R.S., Ch. 1371, Sec. 6, eff. June 15, 2007.

Sec. 38.0181. CARDIOVASCULAR SCREENING PILOT PROGRAM. (a) In this section, "pilot program" means the cardiovascular screening pilot program.

(b) The commissioner shall establish a pilot program under which sixth grade students at participating campuses are administered a cardiovascular screening, including an electrocardiogram and an echocardiogram.

(c) The commissioner shall select campuses to participate in the pilot program. In selecting campuses, the commissioner shall ensure that the cardiovascular screening is administered to an ethnically diverse range of students.

(d) The commissioner may accept grants and donations for use in administering the pilot program.

(e) The commissioner shall require a participating campus to provide the results of a student's cardiovascular screening to the student's parent or guardian.

(f) Expired.

(g) The commissioner may adopt rules necessary to administer this section.

Added by Acts 2007, 80th Leg., R.S., Ch. 1371, Sec. 6, eff. June 15, 2007.

Renumbered from Education Code, Section 38.019 by Acts 2009, 81st Leg., R.S., Ch. 87, Sec. 27.001(6), eff. September 1, 2009.

Sec. 38.019. IMMUNIZATION AWARENESS PROGRAM. (a) A school district that maintains an Internet website shall post prominently on the website:

(1) a list, in English and Spanish, of:

(A) the immunizations required for admission to public school by rules of the Department of State Health Services adopted under Section 38.001;

(B) any immunizations or vaccines recommended for public school students by the Department of State Health Services; and

(C) health clinics in the district that offer the influenza vaccine, to the extent those clinics are known to the district; and

(2) a link to the Department of State Health Services Internet website where a person may obtain information relating to the procedures for claiming an exemption from the immunization requirements of Section 38.001.

(a-1) The link to the Department of State Health Services Internet website provided under Subsection (a)(2) must be presented in the same manner as the information provided under Subsection (a)(1).

(b) The list of recommended immunizations or vaccines under Subsection (a)(2) must include the influenza vaccine, unless the Department of State Health Services requires the influenza vaccine for admission to public school.

Added by Acts 2007, 80th Leg., R.S., Ch. 94, Sec. 3, eff. May 15, 2007.

Sec. 38.022. SCHOOL VISITORS. (a) A school district may require a person who enters a district campus to display the person's driver's license or another form of identification containing the person's photograph issued by a governmental entity.

(b) A school district may establish an electronic database for the purpose of storing information concerning visitors to district campuses. Information stored in the electronic database may be used only for the purpose of school district security and may not be sold or otherwise disseminated to a third party for any purpose.

(c) A school district may verify whether a visitor to a district campus is a sex offender registered with the computerized central database maintained by the Department of Public Safety as provided by Article 62.005, Code of Criminal Procedure, or any other database accessible by the district.

(d) The board of trustees of a school district shall adopt a policy regarding the action to be taken by the administration of a school campus when a visitor is identified as a sex offender.

Added by Acts 2007, 80th Leg., R.S., Ch. 1372, Sec. 12, eff. June 15, 2007.

Sec. 38.023. LIST OF RESOURCES CONCERNING INTERNET SAFETY. The agency shall develop and make available to school districts a list of resources concerning Internet safety, including a list of organizations and Internet websites that may assist in educating teachers and students about:

(1) the potential dangers of allowing personal information to appear on an Internet website;

(2) the significance of copyright laws; and

(3) the consequences of cyber-plagiarism and theft of audiovisual works, including motion pictures, software, and sound recordings, through uploading and downloading files on the Internet.

Added by Acts 2007, 80th Leg., R.S., Ch. 751, Sec. 1, eff. June 15, 2007.

Sec. 38.024. INSURANCE AGAINST STUDENT INJURIES. (a) In compliance with this section, the board of trustees of a school district may obtain insurance against bodily injuries sustained by students while training for or engaging in interschool athletic competition or while engaging in school-sponsored activities on a school campus.

(b) The amount of insurance to be obtained must be in keeping with the financial condition of the school district and may not exceed the amount that, in the opinion of the board of trustees, is reasonably necessary to afford adequate medical treatment of injured students.

(c) The insurance authorized by this section must be obtained from a reliable insurance company authorized to do business in this state and must be on forms approved by the commissioner of insurance.

(d) The cost of the insurance is a legitimate part of the total cost of operating the school district.

(e) The failure of any board of trustees to carry the insurance authorized by this section may not be construed as placing any legal liability on the school district or its officers, agents, or employees for any injury that results.

Added by Acts 1995, 74th Leg., ch. 260, Sec. 1, eff. May 30, 1995. Amended by Acts 2001, 77th Leg., ch. 534, Sec. 1, eff. Sept. 1, 2001.
Transferred from Education Code, Section 33.085 by Acts 2009, 81st Leg., R.S., Ch. 87, Sec. 7.004(a), eff. September 1, 2009.
Amended by:
Acts 2009, 81st Leg., R.S., Ch. 87, Sec. 7.004(b), eff. September 1, 2009.

Sec. 38.026. GRANT PROGRAM FOR BEST PRACTICES IN NUTRITION EDUCATION. (a) The Department of Agriculture shall develop a program under which the department awards grants to public school campuses for best practices in nutrition education.

(b) The Department of Agriculture may solicit and accept gifts, grants, and donations from any public or private source for the purposes of this section.

(c) The Department of Agriculture may adopt rules as necessary to administer a grant program established under this section.

Added by Acts 2009, 81st Leg., R.S., Ch. 728, Sec. 2, eff. June 19, 2009.

Appendix C

State Statutory Code Excerpts regarding Teacher-Student Relations

Nevada Revised Statutes (Excerpt)

Chapter 200—Crimes against the Person

Sexual Assault and Seduction

NRS 200.364 Definitions. As used in NRS 200.364 to 200.3784, inclusive, unless the context otherwise requires:

1. "Offense involving a pupil" means any of the following offenses:

(a) Sexual conduct between certain employees of a school or volunteers at a school and a pupil pursuant to NRS 201.540.

(b) Sexual conduct between certain employees of a college or university and a student pursuant to NRS 201.550.

2. "Perpetrator" means a person who commits a sexual offense or an offense involving a pupil.

3. "Sexual offense" means any of the following offenses:

(a) Sexual assault pursuant to NRS 200.366.

(b) Statutory sexual seduction pursuant to NRS 200.368.

4. "Sexual penetration" means cunnilingus, fellatio, or any intrusion, however slight, of any part of a person's body or any object manipulated or inserted by a person into the genital or anal openings of the body of another, including sexual intercourse in its ordinary meaning.

5. "Statutory sexual seduction" means:

(a) Ordinary sexual intercourse, anal intercourse, cunnilingus or fellatio committed by a person 18 years of age or older with a person under the age of 16 years; or

(b) Any other sexual penetration committed by a person 18 years of age or older with a person under the age of 16 years with the intent of arousing, appealing to, or gratifying the lust or passions or sexual desires of either of the persons.

6. "Victim" means a person who is a victim of a sexual offense or an offense involving a pupil.

(Added to NRS by 1977, 1626; A 1979, 572; 1991, 801; 1995, 700; 2009, 231, 1296)

NRS 200.366 Sexual assault: Definition; penalties.

1. A person who subjects another person to sexual penetration, or who forces another person to make a sexual penetration on himself or herself or another, or on a beast, against the will of

the victim or under conditions in which the perpetrator knows or should know that the victim is mentally or physically incapable of resisting or understanding the nature of his or her conduct, is guilty of sexual assault.

2. Except as otherwise provided in subsections 3 and 4, a person who commits a sexual assault is guilty of a category A felony and shall be punished:

(a) If substantial bodily harm to the victim results from the actions of the defendant committed in connection with or as a part of the sexual assault, by imprisonment in the state prison:

(1) For life without the possibility of parole; or

(2) For life with the possibility of parole, with eligibility for parole beginning when a minimum of 15 years has been served.

(b) If no substantial bodily harm to the victim results, by imprisonment in the state prison for life with the possibility of parole, with eligibility for parole beginning when a minimum of 10 years has been served.

3. Except as otherwise provided in subsection 4, a person who commits a sexual assault against a child under the age of 16 years is guilty of a category A felony and shall be punished:

(a) If the crime results in substantial bodily harm to the child, by imprisonment in the state prison for life without the possibility of parole.

(b) Except as otherwise provided in paragraph (c), if the crime does not result in substantial bodily harm to the child, by imprisonment in the state prison for life with the possibility of parole, with eligibility for parole beginning when a minimum of 25 years has been served.

(c) If the crime is committed against a child under the age of 14 years and does not result in substantial bodily harm to the child, by imprisonment in the state prison for life with the possibility of parole, with eligibility for parole beginning when a minimum of 35 years has been served.

4. A person who commits a sexual assault against a child under the age of 16 years and who has been previously convicted of:

(a) A sexual assault pursuant to this section or any other sexual offense against a child; or

(b) An offense committed in another jurisdiction that, if committed in this State, would constitute a sexual assault pursuant to this section or any other sexual offense against a child, is guilty of a category A felony and shall be punished by imprisonment in the state prison for life without the possibility of parole.

5. For the purpose of this section, "other sexual offense against a child" means any act committed by an adult upon a child constituting:

(a) Incest pursuant to NRS 201.180;

(b) Lewdness with a child pursuant to NRS 201.230;

(c) Sado-masochistic abuse pursuant to NRS 201.262; or

(d) Luring a child using a computer, system or network pursuant to NRS 201.560, if punished as a felony.

(Added to NRS by 1977, 1626; A 1991, 612; 1995, 1186; 1997, 1179, 1719; 1999, 431; 2003, 2825; 2005, 2874; 2007, 3255)

NRS 200.368 Statutory sexual seduction: Penalties. Except under circumstances where a greater penalty is provided in NRS 201.540, a person who commits statutory sexual seduction shall be punished:

1. If the person is 21 years of age or older, for a category C felony as provided in NRS 193.130.

2. If the person is under the age of 21 years, for a gross misdemeanor.

(Added to NRS by 1977, 1627; A 1979, 1426; 1995, 1187; 2001, 703)

Texas Penal Code (Excerpt)

Title 5. Offenses against the Person
Chapter 21. Sexual Offenses

Sec. 21.12. IMPROPER RELATIONSHIP BETWEEN EDUCATOR AND STUDENT. (a) An employee of a public or private primary or secondary school commits an offense if the employee:

(1) engages in sexual contact, sexual intercourse, or deviate sexual intercourse with a person who is enrolled in a public or private primary or secondary school at which the employee works;

(2) holds a certificate or permit issued as provided by Subchapter B, Chapter 21, Education Code, or is a person who is required to be licensed by a state agency as provided by Section 21.003(b), Education Code, and engages in sexual contact, sexual intercourse, or deviate sexual intercourse with a person the employee knows is:

(A) enrolled in a public primary or secondary school in the same school district as the school at which the employee works; or

(B) a student participant in an educational activity that is sponsored by a school district or a public or private primary or secondary school, if:

(i) students enrolled in a public or private primary or secondary school are the primary participants in the activity; and

(ii) the employee provides education services to those participants; or

(3) engages in conduct described by Section 33.021, with a person described by Subdivision (1), or a person the employee knows is a person described by Subdivision (2)(A) or (B), regardless of the age of that person.

(b) An offense under this section is a felony of the second degree.

(b-1) It is an affirmative defense to prosecution under this section that:

(1) the actor was the spouse of the enrolled person at the time of the offense; or

(2) the actor was not more than three years older than the enrolled person and, at the time of the offense, the actor and the enrolled person were in a relationship that began before the actor's employment at a public or private primary or secondary school.

(c) If conduct constituting an offense under this section also constitutes an offense under another section of this code, the actor may be prosecuted under either section or both sections.

(d) The name of a person who is enrolled in a public or private primary or secondary school and involved in an improper relationship with an educator as provided by Subsection (a) may not be released to the public and is not public information under Chapter 552, Government Code.

Added by Acts 2003, 78th Leg., ch. 224, Sec. 1, eff. Sept. 1, 2003.
Amended by:

Acts 2007, 80th Leg., R.S., Ch. 610, Sec. 1, eff. September 1, 2007.
Acts 2007, 80th Leg., R.S., Ch. 772, Sec. 1, eff. September 1, 2007.
Acts 2009, 81st Leg., R.S., Ch. 260, Sec. 2, eff. September 1, 2009.
Acts 2011, 82nd Leg., R.S., Ch. 761, Sec. 3, eff. September 1, 2011.

References and Recommended Resources

References

Barley, Z. A., and A. D. Beesley. 2007. Rural school success: What can we learn? *Journal of Research in Rural Education* 22 (1): 1–22. http://jrre.psu.edu/articles/22-1.pdf.

Cotton, K. 1996. School size, school climate, and student performance. www.apexsql.com/_brian/School%20Size%20Matters.pdf.

Raywid, M. A. 1996. *Taking stock: The movement to create mini-schools, schools-within-schools, and separate small schools.* New York: ERIC Clearinghouse on Urban Education. www.eric.ed.gov/PDFS/ED396045.pdf.

Viadero, D. 2010. Study finds success in NYC's "small schools." *Education Week* 29 (36): 5. www.edweek.org/ew/articles/2010/06/23/36nyc.h29.html.

Wasley, P. A., and R. J. Lear. 2001. Small schools, real gains. *Educational Leadership Magazine* 58 (6): 22–27.

Recommended Resources

Classification Systems for Learning and Teaching

Erickson, H. L. 2002. *Concept-based curriculum and instruction: Teaching beyond the facts.* Thousand Oaks, CA: Corwin Press.

———. 2006. *Concept-based curriculum and instruction for the thinking classroom.* Thousand Oaks, CA: Corwin Press.

Marzano, R., and Kendall, J. 2007. *The new taxonomy of educational objectives*. Thousand Oaks, CA: Corwin Press.

———. 2008. *Designing and assessing educational objectives: Applying the new taxonomy*. Thousand Oaks, CA: Corwin Press.

School Safety and SRO Programs

Center for the Prevention of School Violence, North Carolina Department of Juvenile Justice and Delinquency Prevention. SRO job description. www.ncdjjdp.org/cpsv/sro/job_description.html.

COPS (Community Oriented Policing Services, US Department of Justice). School safety toolkit. www.cops.usdoj.gov/Default.asp?Item=1588.

Crisis Prevention Institute. www.crisisprevention.com.

Maryland Association of School Resource Officers. www.masro.com.

National Association of School Resources Officers. www.nasro.org.

National Institute of Justice. School safety: Programs and planning. www.nij.gov/topics/crime/school-crime/school-safety/welcome.htm.

Randy Sprick's Safe and Civil Schools. www.safeandcivilschools.com.

Texas Association of School Resource Officers. http://tasro.org.

Preparing for Crises

Braud, G. School crisis communication plans. www.schoolcrisisplan.com.

FEMA, US Department of Homeland Security. 2011. *Sample school emergency operations plan*. www.training.fema.gov/EMIWeb/emischool/EL361Toolkit/assets/SamplePlan.pdf.

Fort Hood, US Army. Sample poster of area resources with telephone numbers. www.killeenisd.org/schoolDocs/c117/documents/FortHoodAreaResources.pdf.

Killeen (Texas) Independent School District. Sample letter to parents regarding the district's regarding emergency planning and response actions. www.killeenisd.org/departmentDocs/c933/documents/EmergencyOpsParentActions.pdf.

Lead and Manage My School, US Department of Education. Campus security. www2.ed.gov/admins/lead/safety/campus.html.

———. Emergency planning. www2.ed.gov/admins/lead/safety/emergencyplan/index.html.

National School Safety and Security Services. School crisis and school emergency plans. www.schoolsecurity.org/resources/crisis.html.

Office of Postsecondary Education, US Department of Education. 2011. *The handbook for campus safety and security reporting.* www2.ed.gov/admins/lead/safety/handbook.pdf.

 **LAURA TRUJILLO-JENKS** earned an associate's degree from the New Mexico Military Institute, a bachelor's degree from the University of Texas at Austin, a master's degree from Austin Peay State University in Tennessee, and a PhD in educational administration at UT Austin. She has served in several capacities in public education, including teacher, special education coordinator, assistant principal, and principal in school districts in Texas, Colorado, and Kentucky. At the University of North Texas at Dallas, she taught courses in the Educational Administration program and served on the Faculty Alliance/Senate as both secretary and chair-elect.

Currently, Laura is an assistant professor in the Department of Teacher Education at Texas Woman's University, where she teaches courses in the Educational Leadership program, including educational law. She is the author of *Survival Guide for New Teachers: How to Become a Professional, Effective, and Successful Teacher* and an associate editor for the *Journal of Cases in Educational Leadership*. Her research centers on both campus leadership and campus safety through effective student discipline, and she is passionately interested in educational law, school safety, and healthy human organizations.

 **MINERVA TRUJILLO** retired from the Killeen Independent School District after 35 years of service, including 29 years dedicated to the students of KISD as a teacher, an assistant principal, a coordinator for certified personnel, and the principal of Willow Springs Elementary School, Maxdale Elementary School, and Audie Murphy Middle School. As an army wife, she traveled throughout the United States and Europe and taught in Germany, New Mexico, Kentucky, and Kansas before coming to the Fort Hood area. She earned a bachelor's degree at Eastern New Mexico University in Portales and a master's at Auburn University in Alabama.

Minerva has received numerous awards and honors from organizations such as the Killeen NAACP Youth Council, the Hispanic-American Chamber of Commerce of Central Texas, the Region 12 Association of Texas Professional Educators, the Killeen Classroom Teachers Association, the Girl Scouts, and Fort Hood. She currently serves as a member of the KISD Board of Trustees, the Killeen Housing Authority Board of Commissioners, the Board Development Committee of Girls Scouts of Central Texas, and the Communities In Schools Board of Directors.

To order other products from Park Place Publications and its subsidiaries, visit www.legaldigest.com